Angels in Africa

5/29/05

Dear Cindy & Wayne,

God bless you
in the weekend of
celebrating your mother-
77th birthday and as
57th Anniversary.

Lots of love,

Mom Dad Dillon

Psalm 91:11
Isaiah 58:04

Angels in Africa

The Founding of Ghana Christian College

Dr. Jerry Gibson

To order additional copies of this book, contact:
Xlibris Corporation
1-888-795-4274
www.Xlibris.com
Orders@Xlibris.com
24650

GHANA CHRISTIAN
UNIVERSITY
(FORMERLY GHANA CHRISTIAN COLLEGE & SEMINARY)

37th
Annual Graduation

Guest of Honour:
His Excellency Mr. J. A. Kufuor
President of the Republic of Ghana

Date: Saturday, 9th August, 2003 Time: 10am prompt.
Venue: New Campus, Amrahia, Dodowa Road, Accra

Contents

Acknowledgements

We would like to dedicate this book to the memory of two great soldiers of the cross, Max Ward Randall and Cyril Simkins, who were pioneers in the establishment of Ghana Christian College. They traveled through Ghana in the early Nineteen Sixties and brought back the report of a need for a college in Ghana to train African ministers and evangelists. They were the ones whose words, more than any others, motivated us to reluctantly respond, "Here am I, send me."

We further acknowledge our Son in the Lord, Michael Mcfadden for his untiring work with our computer that made possible the completion of our manuscript. We could not have done it without him. We also acknowledge Craig Melville and Brad Gomer, for their technical assistance.

We give special thanks to Victor Pearn, whose efforts made possible the publishing of our first book, "Worth Any Sacrifice", and this book also. He served as the editor of both books and made a valuable contribution that only he could make. I had the privilege of writing the back cover on his book, "American Western Song" which was nominated for a Pulitzer Prize. His book, "Devil Dogs and Jar Heads" should be read by everybody who has ever been in the military service of our country, as well as those who have had loved ones there. We acknowledge once again Noah and Ruth Marcum for encouraging us to write about our experiences with angels. We give special thanks to Dena Baker for her excellent work as the artist for the cover of this book. Finally, we acknowledge my immediate family. Normadeene and the children made the greatest sacrifice of all. And they are the ones who the Ghanaians will remember the most, of whom they said, "They loved us too much!"

Preface

"THEY LOVED US TOO MUCH!"

Fools for Christ

This book is a natural sequel to "Worth Any Sacrifice". As we suggested at the close of that book, the first forty years of our lives served well to prepare us for the work we were called to accomplish in Africa. We have told our students through the years that in direct proportion to how we prepare ourselves, God will open avenues of service for us. I would rather have a student die before he preached his first sermon than to go out unprepared. The Word of God is described as "a two edged sword." Hebrews 4: 12. A sharp, two edged sword can do an awfully lot of damage in the wrong hands. That is especially true of a child.

The mission that prompted the writing of this book was to establish a college in Ghana, West Africa for the training of Ghanaian ministers and evangelists. It was a true example of a definition given for a "missionary". A missionary is said to be someone who goes where he or she has not been, to do what they have not done, with money they do not have. That was indeed the case with us.

We were called back to Ghana twenty five years later to help celebrate the Silver Anniversary of

Ghana Christian College and Seminary. Words can not express the joy that filled our hearts as we observed the growth of the college from the time of its inception in 1966. It humbled us deeply when we were taken to one of the dormitories named Gibson Hall. And then, after 37 years, seeing "Ghana Christian University.

As we look back, we understand more than ever the truth in the words, "Fools rush in where angels fear to tread." Selling your home and most of your worldly possessions, and uprooting your four children, three teen agers and a seven year old girl, from their friends and schools, and leaving for a destination that was very unfriendly to Christian, and especially, white Christians, seemed very foolish to our friends and family. We were told it was not fair for us to take our children to Africa. Several of our missionaries had been recently killed, and the President of Ghana, Kwami Nkrumah hated white people, especially white Christians.

These words are not original with me, but I used them often when confronted by friends and family in regard to our foolishness in taking our children to Africa. "Can a man be considered 'foolish' for giving up that which he can not keep, in exchange for that which he can not lose?" Yes, we were fools alright, but like the Apostle Paul, we were fools for Christ." II Corinthians 12:11.

My brother Harlow was in the back seat of our car some time before we left for Ghana. He was expounding on how foolish and dangerous it was to take our children to a place like Ghana, Africa. Our youngest son, G.A. interrupted him and asked, "But what about all of those souls in Africa?" That was the last time Harlow spoke against our mission to Ghana. I often remind people that *the safest place for a Christian to be, is where God wants him to be."*

We had some close calls. Our children were often near the jaws of death. However, as you will see as you read this book, God's angels were willing to tread with us and were there for us when we needed them the most. Perhaps the most memorable and meaningful words expressed to us while in Ghana, were the words of an old man at the hospital in Kumasi, when we thought we might lose G.A. because of a terrible accident. Normadeene watched helplessly, as the Ghanaian nurses tried to make G.A. comfortable until a doctor could attend him. The old man placed his hand on her shoulder and simply said, "Mama, God can take our bad times and turn them into good times." The truth in those words sustained us the rest of the time we were in Ghana. Romans 8:28 says the same. "God causes all things to work together for good, for those who love Him, and are called according to His purpose." Normadeene certainly was qualified in this respect, as she has always loved God dearly and has had one goal in life, and that is to please Him.

Please join us "fools for Christ," as we take you on an adventure of a life time, that served to change the lives of many people through the past thirty five or so years. The first half of our lives called for many worth while sacrifices. The beginning of the second half, as you well see, called for even greater sacrifices. But it was worth it all. You will agree when you hear one of our Ghanaian students, who is now the President of the college say, "They loved us too much!"

Gale and Don Earl Boatman, long time
friends of Jerry and Normadeene Gibson.
Don Earl is a retired President of
Ozark Christian College.

Chapter I

THE LETTERS

It was Indian summer for the Gibson family. "God surely must be pleased with us," we thought. Things could not be better for our family individually and collectively. The children were happy and doing well in school. We had just built the house of our dreams in Crystal New Hope, a new suburb of Minneapolis. We were working to help establish a church in St. Louis Park, west of Minneapolis, the Knollwood Church of Christ. Yes, God certainly must be pleased with us.

On top of all of this I was in line for a Sabbatical leave from Minnesota Bible College, having been there for ten years. I had been approached by Dr. D. Douglas Young, a professor from Northwest Bible College, to join him in a venture in Jerusalem teaching Hebrew and perhaps helping to decipher The Dead Sea Scrolls. I was very excited about that prospect and felt very honored to be chosen for such a task. Don't you agree? God certainly must have been *very* pleased with us. We failed to mention that we had also realized a long time dream of establishing a campus ministry on the University of Minnesota campus. For several years I had watched hundreds or perhaps thousands of young men and women from my class room's corner window, crossing University

Avenue to attend their classes at the university. I wondered where they were in relationship to their Creator or if they had any real purpose in life. I was on the staff of Dean Williamson, the Student Dean of the University and worked with Dr. Henry Allen and the Religious Workers Association. This opened many doors for me that had been closed to our college since its inception. Then came the first of several letters that were destined to change our immediate plans as well as the destiny of our lives, and the lives of many others.

In the fall of 1964 we received a letter from Cyril Simkins who at the time was working with Mashoko Bible College in what was then known as Northern Rhodesia. He told of how he and several other missionaries had been invited to Ghana, West Africa by a group of Churches who had united under the title Universal Christian Church. Along with Cyril Simkins were Max Ward Randall and I believe Edgar Nichols. Noteworthy Africans that traveled with them were John Quansa, Moses Adai and J.C.K. Hayford. He told us that there was a great need for a Bible college in West Africa that could train African ministers and evangelists for ministry. He closed his letter by asking us to pray that God would raise the right man or men who would be willing to answer the call to such a ministry.

Having been a professor at the Bible College, for what at the time seemed many years and being well known among our churches and colleges, we thought he wanted us to help find such a man. We immediately started to think of men and women we thought may be both qualified and interested in filling such a need.

Then came the second letter. This time it was from Max Ward Randall, a veteran missionary to Africa whose son and daughter were students of mine at Minnesota Bible College. Max Randall started with the words, "By this time you most likely have received a letter from my good friend Cyril Simkins." He continued to tell us of the opportunity that existed in Ghana for spreading the Gospel of Jesus Christ to a people who were eager to hear and respond to the message. He said the people of Ghana "Have a tremendous hunger for the truth." He went on to say that he had never met people who were more Spirit filled. He said, "As Cyril Simkins has already informed you, we are looking for a man or a family who would come to Ghana and help establish a Christian college." We thought he wanted us to recommend somebody. We figured his son and daughter had told him about our interest in world-wide missions, and thought that after having time to think about it, we may be able to recommend somebody.

Then came the shock, as well as words that were destined to change our lives for ever. He asked, "Would you and your wife be interested in going to Ghana to establish such a college?"

My name immediately changed from Jerry Gibson to "Jonah" Gibson. There was no way that I would ever consider taking my wife and family to the jungles of Africa! One of our missionaries had just been killed in the Congo. I had chuckled over a cartoon I had recently seen depicting two cannibals discussing a missionary one of them had just eaten. It was a Roman Catholic missionary. One of the cannibals said, "That was the toughest missionary I have ever eaten." The other inquired as to how he had prepared him. He replied, "I boiled him." To which the other cannibal responded, "No wonder he was tough, he was supposed be a Friar." Those were the crazy kinds of thoughts that rushed through my mind.

We wrote to Max Randall and explained to him that we had other plans so it would be impossible for us to accept the invitation to go to Ghana at that time. However, we assured him we would do all that was within our power to help them find the right man for the task.

Up until that time we were sure that God was well pleased with us. Everything seemed to be just right for our family. Suddenly all of that changed. I had every reason to be happy and have a joyful spirit. But that was not the case. I became irritable and just plain miserable. I could not sleep and everything seemed to be going wrong. I tried to talk to myself, but that didn't seem to lift my spirit. Down deep in my heart I knew what was wrong. Like Jonah, I was "sanctified in spots." I was running away from what I knew was God's will for my life.

Suddenly one night I woke out of a troubled sleep and shook Normadeene and said, "If they still want us, we will go to Ghana!" It was like a great load off of our shoulders. Once again we felt God's strong hand on us. We knew God was pleased with our decision and that He would continue to take very good care of us.

Some months after informing Max Randall of our decision to accept the invitation to go to Ghana, and after we started to make preparations for this new "leap of faith," we received the following letter from the General Secretary of the Universal Christian Church. Max had informed them of our desire to help. It proved to confirm the fact that we had made the right decision.

J.H.O. Nelson
C/O P.O. Box 1977
Kumasi, Ghana, West Africa
October 25, 1965

Dear Professor Gibson,

Choicest Christian greetings to you from a Christian brother on the battlefield for Christ in Ghana Africa.

It is my great pleasure as the General Secretary of the Universal Christian Church in Ghana to be able to reach you there this day in these few words.

It is quite a long time since we heard of you and I am therefore directed by the pastors and all members of the Universal Christian Church in Ghana to inform you that we are eagerly awaiting you coming to work with us here in Ghana.

I want to assure you that these saints have confidence in you, and believe your presence here will be of very great benefit to us all and our country as a whole both spiritually and physically.

Brother Edgar Nichols is here with us, but that is in no way going to hinder you coming.

We have learnt to love you ever since we heard of your great interest in the Gospel of work in Africa. We love to have you here in our midst. And are looking forward to the time God will direct.

You may be surprised to hear perhaps for the first time, that Brother J.C.K. Hayford has been dismissed from the Universal Christian Church in Ghana for bad conduct. We are very sorry for that but it was a thing we could not help.

And his hard heartedness and unrepentant spirit nearly caused the fall of the whole church, but our Heavenly Father in His wise council saved the situation. All is well now. Many souls have been added to the Church.

Brother Gibson, the work is great on this part of the globe, and it requires men with the Holy Spirit and with great compassion for lost souls! Thousands of our fellow brethren are lost in sin, hopelessly heading towards a Christ less damnation. The only hope for them lies in Christ. But who can and will help them to find Christ? Christ must be preached to the lost on our continent now or never!

We need the Gospel preached in all its nakedness. The truth of Jesus Christ must be revealed to the lost world! Professor, I beg to entreat you and your family to treat this all important matter urgently. Pray earnestly for the work of Christ here. Pray again about your desire to come over here with the Gospel and seek Him for his own direction.

Prepare, for we are waiting for you. Be sure of your coming without fear, for you will receive co-operation from people of like faith and practice.

We are praying for you and your family, and we hope to see you at no distant date.

Hoping to hear from you very soon,
Thank you and God bless you.
Yours in Christ,

J.H.O. Nelson

There was a sense of urgency in J.H,O. Nelson's letter as you may well agree. From the time we made the decision to answer the Macedonian Call from The Universal Christian Church in Ghana, we immediately started to face the challenges before us. You don't just pick up and leave for Africa. We never imagined how difficult it would be to finally arrive on the soil of Ghana, West Africa.

Since returning from Africa, we prepared a pamphlet entitled, "So you want to be a Missionary" that explains many of the things that are necessary in preparation for such a venture. It deals with such things as passports, visas, health certificates, Forwarding Agents, letters of credit for establishing bank account, transportation and housing after you arrive on the mission field. We wish we had possessed this information before we went. We have helped many missionary candidates to avoid unnecessary difficulties by placing our pamphlet in their hands. Let us start form the beginning and consider that fact that man proposes, but it is God who disposes, or in other words, God's time is the best time. We wanted to leave for Ghana right away. Letters like the one we received from J. O. Nelson served to intensify that desire. However, we had some very important lessons to learn, such as *the blessings of waiting.*

Cyril Simkins with Joseph Hayford and
leaders of The Universal Christian Church

Max Ward Randall, Pioneer Missionary to
Ghana with Joseph Hayford & African
leaders of the Universal Christian Church

Chapter II

THE BLESSINGS OF WAITING

(The battle of the visa)

"I waited patiently for the Lord, and He
inclined unto me and heard my cry,
" Psalms 40:1

We were about to begin *the long wait*. I informed
Howard Hayes, the Academic Dean of Minnesota Bible
College, of our decision to forego our invitation from
Douglas Young to work with him in Israel, and
instead accept the call to establish a Christian College
in Ghana, West Africa. We realized that that might
require extending my Sabbatical leave an extra year,
which would not be easy. They would have to find
someone to take over my classes in Old Testament
and Evangelism for an additional year. It was
destined to meet fierce opposition, as it would make
necessary postponing the Sabbatical Leave of the
person next in line. All of this eventually proved to
be true. Dean Hayes had a tremendous passion for
missions, and was one hundred percent behind our
decision. He vowed to do whatever was needed to
make possible the success of our mission to Ghana.
He was true to his word, as the long wait for a visa
made extending our Sabbatical Leave absolutely
necessary. Without his enthusiastic lobbying of "the

powers to be" from Minnesota Bible College, we could
never have gone to Ghana.

I believe this would be a good time to share an
experience we had with Howard Hayes. Howard was
raised in the mountains of Tennessee. He had a
great love for guns. He bought a Colt revolver from a
University Student, and showed it off to me in his
new office. He had recently been named Academic
Dean for Minnesota Bible College. The two of us had
often had target practice at a local gravel pit. He
had a dead eye with a gun. His office was furnished
with a new filing cabinet, desk, swivel chair and an
unabridged dictionary. He bragged to me about the
good deal he had made a the student who needed
money badly and sold the gun to him for far less
that it was worth.

He then looked at me and said, "You need a gun
like this to take with you to Africa," I asked him,
"What for?" He replied, "To shoot snakes, rats and
maybe even spiders." I could tell by the tone of his
voice that he was dead serious. I took him seriously,
so decided to go to a nearby sports shop and see
what kind of guns they had for sale.

I handled many guns. I wanted one that felt good
in my hand. They tried to sell me a little Derringer,
but I decided that would not be practical. I finally
decided on a little twenty two caliber Steven Pistol. I
purchased a box of longs shells and a box of short
shells. The clerk called to me before I left the store
and asked if I wanted to buy a box of what he called
acorn shells. They had the same size casing, but a
very small bullet. He said these would be great for
shooting rats and such like. I purchased a box of
them.

I drove back to the college and went immediately
to Dean Hayes' office. I showed him my new pistol,

and also the shells I had purchased for it. He was delighted to see it. His eyes sparkled as he fumbled with the cartridge cylinder. He then did a strange thing. He grabbed the box of acorn shells from my hand and proceeded to load the pistol. He took a piece of paper and pasted it on his new unabridged dictionary and placed it on his new filing cabinet. He stepped back, raised the pistol, and fired point blank at the make shift target on his filing cabinet. The report from that little acorn shell sounded like a shot from a canon. It shot a hole in Dean Hayes' unabridged dictionary all the way to the L and Ms. I could not believe what I just witnessed. Dean Hayes was a very dignified college professor. This was completely out of character for him. I will never forget the look of unbelief on his face. I lost it. I almost rolled on the floor of his office with laughter. He begged me to keep what had happened a secret. Little did we know what the future had in store for that little, seemingly harmless twenty two caliber pistol, that could shoot acorn type shells. More important to us at the time, was taking care of the business necessary for us to be able to move to Africa.

There was also the matter of what to do with our beautiful new house with all of its furnishings. We hated to think about having to sell it. But we thought that might be easier than trying to find a suitable tenant to rent it. And what to do with the hundreds of items we had accumulated through our almost twenty years of marriage? Where would we store all of these things? I never throw anything away. I would take some of my books with me, but I had hundreds of book in my library that would have to be kept safe while we were gone.

Then there was the matter of obtaining six visas from the Ghanaian Embassy. That required obtaining passports for each member of our family. That made necessary obtaining six passport size photos for each of us to be placed in our passports and visas. Along with these we had to include International Certificates of Vaccination. That meant we would soon have to begin a series of very painful shots for such things as Yellow Fever and Cholera. Our biggest danger was with Malaria, but there were no shots available for that. I didn't relish the thought of all of those shots, as I have always hated to be stuck with needles. In short, I hate pain!

We would have to obtain the necessary documents to be filled out in triplicate, along with a letter of credit from a bank in America. These were all to be accompanied by an official letter of invitation from a recognized religious body in Ghana. We did all of the above. Then began *the battle of the visa* and *the long wait!*

We sent our passports along with the necessary documents to the Counsel General of Ghana located in New York City. Everything was in order. We thought it would be a matter of a few short weeks before we would receive our passports back from the Ghanaian Counsel General along with our visas stamped and ready to go. In the mean time, we decided it would be better for us to sell our home rather than rent it to somebody. We knew a young married couple, the Kenneth Hoefts, from Kimball, Minnesota who were living in a small house trailer. They had expressed a desire to buy our house. However, they would have to sell their trailer in order to have the necessary down payment. After much prayer, they were able to find a buyer. They wanted to close the deal with us and move into their new home as soon as possible. We agreed to let them take over the payments on our G. 1. loan and work out the details with the bank that held our mortgage. Thinking we would receive our visas in a short time, we decided to leave most of the furnishings with them, store what was left at the college, and find a motel to live in. We were able to rent a room with a small kitchen at The Royal Crown Motel next to the Crystal Airport in Crystal-New Hope. It was a pretty tight squeeze for the six of us, but we only planned to be there a couple of weeks at the most. There were two double beds for the children in the main room and a roll away for Normadeene and me in the small kitchen, God was about to do a work in our lives in regard to the virtue of *patience.* Each day we would go to our mail box at the college to see if our visas had arrived. This went on for days that turned into weeks and then into months. It became embarrassing for us, as each day people would ask, "Are you still here?" All of this time my Sabbatical was being eaten away. People began to doubt that we would ever obtain a visa.

It so happened that the then President of Ghana, Kwame Nkrumah had a hatred for America where he attended college. He was an atheistic Communist and hated Christians as well as Americans. He was not about to let a visa to be granted to a Christian family whose mission was to establish a Christian college in his country.

During this time of waiting, we kept as busy as possible preparing for our mission in Ghana. I purchased a Rocket Duplicator and prepared lecture notes and other educational materials that would prove to be very valuable after we arrived in Ghana.

We also needed to build a financial base of support for our mission. I was receiving half salary from the college and would have to have money to supplement that for our family's personal needs. I would also have to raise money for our Service link that would take care of the expenses for the college.

We decided to recruit what we called Lieutenants for Christ. We figured that we would need eight-hundred and seventy-five dollars a month to take care of our Living link and Service link. So we appealed to one-hundred individuals as well as churches to commit eight dollars and seventy-five cents per month as Lieutenants for Christ. Breaking it down into small increments gave many people an opportunity to share in our mission in Ghana. However, even this was very difficult as people did not want to commit themselves financially to a cause many thought to be futile. They believed Kwame Nkrumah would never grant us our visas. We were beginning to have our doubts too. They suggested his government would have to be overthrown before we would be given visas, and that seemed hardly likely. Then came a much needed boost for our faith.

One evening our family decided to take in a movie. Ben Hur was playing at a theatre on Broadway Avenue in North Minneapolis. We were getting *stir crazy* living in the cramped quarters of The Royal Crown Motel. In fact, due to the crowded conditions in the motel, we took Cindy down to Clarion, Iowa to live with Normadeene's mother. She enrolled in Clarion Senior High School. That proved to be a costly mistake, as Cindy believed that we did not love her and were trying to get rid of her. The experience proved to be very negative with future consequences. Hindsight is certainly better than foresight. If we had it do over again, we would have kept her there with us regardless of the over crowded conditions.

We parked across the street from the theatre near the corner of Broadway Avenue. It was a busy intersection with stop lights. We were driving an old green Ford station wagon. With the aid of the stop lights we walked across the street to the theatre. The movie was just what we needed. It got our minds off of the battle of the visas and served to be a source of encouragement. Since then, we have seen the movie many times.

As we walked out of the theatre Becky, our seven year old, saw our station wagon across the street. She broke away from us and dashed out into the street to run across to it. Just then a large truck came speeding through the stop light which had just turned green. Becky did not see it coming. She was running right into its path! We stood there in horror visualizing her little body being tossed into the air by that speeding piece of steel. In our minds she was as good as dead. Just as she was about to run into the path of the truck something grabbed her by the shoulders and pulled her back out of the way. Her blond hair flew in the air as the truck brushed close by her. It was our angel! Once again God proved to be true to His promises in Psalms 91:11, "I will give my angels charge over you." And also, I Corinthians 10:13 which says, "There has no temptation taken you, but what is common to man. *But God is* faithful, who will not allow you to be tempted beyond we are able, but will with the temptation provide a way of escape so that we will be able to bear it." Had Becky been killed that night, God knew it would be a burden too great for us to bear, and we most likely would never have gone to Ghana.

Normadeene heard on the radio that Kwame Nkrumah had traveled to China to meet Chairman

Mao. She prayed that something would happen while
he was out of the country. The next morning we heard
on the radio that a coup had overthrown the Nkrumah
government. God had heard and answered
Normadeene's prayer. Since that time I have told
many people that if Normadeene would pray that
the ceiling in this room would fall down I would get
out of the building immediately,

The very next week, on May 4th, my birthday, we
received our residence visas, the first that had been
granted for some time. And on May 26th,
Normadeene's birthday, we met under the dome in
Minnesota Bible College's chapel in a prayer circle
with many of our friends. They presented
Normadeene with a beautiful birthday cake. We then
sang, "So Send I You." And they sent us on our way
to accomplish our mission in Ghana. The experience
of waiting for our visas proved very valuable to us. It
not only gave us time to prepare valuable educational
materials and build a financial base for our mission,
but it also taught us many other valuable lessons.
Yes, it was difficult. Becky came down with the
measles during that cold winter. Normadeene and I
slept on a three quarter roll away for nine months,
in that little kitchen, with our feet in the oven and
our heads in the refrigerator. We got awfully tired of
having people ask us, "Are you still here?" But, once
again, it was worth any sacrifice we were called upon
to make.

Waiting on the Lord can be a tremendous blessing.
I heard a minister comment on the blessing of
waiting. He said that waiting strengthens our faith.
It intensifies our love, and, it serves to discipline
our behavior. All of these proved to be true for us as
our long wait and the battle of the visas came to a
victorious end.

"I waited patiently for the Lord; And He inclined to me, and heard my cry.
"Psalms 40:1

"But if we hope for what we do not see, with perseverance we wait for it."
Romans 8:25

Minnesota Bible College from where Jerry Gibson & Family took a Sabbatical Leave to establish Ghana Christian College.

Jerry & Normadeene Gibson's home which they sold before leaving for Ghana. (upper left)

Hugh Harrison with his grandson and
son and son-in-laws in front of the
Knollwood Church where Jerry
preached before leaving for Ghana.

Chapter III

THE ADVENTURE BEGINS

Long before we received our visas, we made plans for our journey to Africa. We decided to travel to Ghana by way of England, France and Switzerland. We were informed by the American Express Travel Agent who served as our travel guide that it would not cost any more money for us to take that route, than it would to travel a more direct route. However, there would be additional expenses for food and lodging.

I am a Charter Member of the American Express credit card, which proved to be very valuable to us both going to and from Ghana. We did not have the money to pay for six air fares, and were able to use the American Express extended payment plan, which spread our payments over a twelve month period. We planned to pay it off much sooner, if possible, in order to avoid interest charges. Our travel agent arranged for everything we would need. He booked us into moderately priced hotels and gave us valuable advice concerning tipping and other European customs.

We went to Montgomery Wards in St. Paul and had them ship a refrigerator, large air conditioner, and queen size bed to our port of departure in New York City. This would follow us to Africa as unaccompanied baggage. One of the reasons we chose to travel to Africa by way of Europe was because many of the things we found necessary to take with us, such as books, educational materials, dishes, silver ware, bedding, Bibles, etc., and a twenty-two caliber pistol with several boxes of ammunition would come by way of a surface vessel and would take more than a month to get there. We found a shipping company in Minneapolis that packed and carried our things to New York, and arranged for them, along with our automobile to be shipped to Ghana. We did not know where we would be in Ghana, so we shipped them in care of Elder John Quansah in Takoradi. John Quansah proved to be a valuable friend, as well as a faithful member of The Universal Christian Church that extended the invitation for us to establish the college in Ghana. His address, P.O. Box 01 12, Takoradi, Ghana, West Africa became a source of security for us, as it was the only sure places we could give as an address in Ghana.

We mentioned that we shipped our automobile along with our other unaccompanied baggage. Shortly before we left Minneapolis for New York, we traded the old green Ford station wagon for a 1964 four door Mercury Comet. That was probably the most valuable piece of unaccompanied baggage we brought with us. Had we known then, what we know now, we most likely would have purchased a foreign vehicle, such as a Land Rover, if we could have afforded it. However on our limited budget, the Comet served us well. It was the only one like it in all of Ghana, and the African people recognized us when they saw it. We would advise those who plan to take a vehicle to Africa, to take one that is very rugged to stand the test of unimproved roads that are not maintained. It must have been a sight to see us packing that little Comet for our trip to New York.

We purchased a car top carrier to help us get in all of the things we desired to take with us. We recommend traveling as light as possible. We did not do so. We have pictures of The Comet being loaded outside of the room at The Royal Crown Hotel. Our friends from Minnesota Bible College gave Normadeene a beautiful birthday cake the night before, when we met to pray with them. She carried it on her lap for many miles until we finally consumed it. We have pictures of our boarding airplanes carrying all of the things we brought with us. Each of the children had special things that served as security blankets for them, such as an old doll, a pillow, a dirty old bear, a G.I. Joe footlocker, and such like.

The trip from Minneapolis to New York City was uneventful, other than the questions that were asked over and over again. "When "I are going to get there?" "Are we there yet?" "I have to go to the bathroom!" It seemed that we had to stop at every rest stop on the way. The children were always hungry, and asked "When are we going to eat?" starting five minutes after we had just finished eating.

We decided to visit my brother Harlow and his family in Richmond, Virginia. It was not much out of the way, and it would be our last contact with any of our immediate family until we returned home from Africa. We had a good visit with them, and then left early the next morning with prayer and hugs and kisses.

Our route from Richmond took us right through Washington D.C. on Pennsylvania Avenue. We stopped in front of the White House and took pictures which we hold very dear to this day. A sense of homesickness had already started to creep into our hearts. We began to appreciate our American heritage more than ever.

Upon arriving in New York City, we booked into our Hotel, and then called our shipping agent. We had allowed for three days of touring New York City, which would include visiting The Statue of Liberty, The Empire State Building, Grand Central Station and Greenwich Village. We had to have the car at the shipping dock by 6:PM. the third day. Time flew by. There were so many sights we were not able to see. When we toured the Statue of Liberty we did not dream that thirty-six years later we would be in Afghanistan with Operation Enduring Freedom. And as we stood on the observation deck of The Empire State Building and looked over the fabulous sky line dotted with gigantic sky scrapers, we never dreamed there would be a *9/11*, for there was no Trade Center in May of 1966.

We managed to drop the car off just in time, and then took a cab back to our hotel. We asked the cab driver to pick us up the, next morning to take us to the airport where we were to fly on Pan American Airlines to London, England. We were now starting to have butterflies in our stomachs. It really hit us. We are actually leaving America. We were actually on our way to the jungles of Ghana, West Africa! We were in for the adventure of our lives!

I took pictures of the children standing in front of the large Pan Am sign in front of the terminal, as well as pictures of them sitting in the airport and boarding the airplane. I wanted to capture the moment, for just such a time as this of sharing our experiences with you.

As the giant Pan Am jet soared out over Manhattan Bay, we praised God for having brought us this far on our mission to Africa. I did not mention it, as we take it for granted, but we saturated our lives with prayer. We prayed without ceasing from the time we accepted the call to go to Ghana, and continued to do so until we arrived back home. We continue to do the same as a habit of our lives every hour of each day. Prayer is our highline that leads to our source of power, Almighty God. It is never out of place for a person to pray. It is like breathing in and breathing out. We know that God will stay by our side if we stay by His side. He will not move. We thought we knew how to pray before we went to Africa. However, we really learned how to pray while we were in Ghana.

The flight attendants treated our family like royalty. They did everything possible to make our flight across the Atlantic both memorable and comfortable. Due to the time change, we would arrive at Heathrow Airport early the next morning. We tried to sleep, but found that impossible. As the jet circled Heathrow Airport we found ourselves wide awake. As we left the airplane, the children with one accord announced, "We're hungry!"

Minnesota Bible College family picnic for the
Gibsons before they left for Ghana.

G.A. & Becky in front of the Royal Crown
Motel where the Gibsons lived
while waiting for a visa.

The Gibsons in front of their Royal Crown
Motel room before leaving for Ghana.

Normadeene with Gibby, Cindy, G.A. and
Beck with her bear in front of the Comet all
packed and ready for the trip to New York.

Normadeene with her birthday cake given to
her by the MBC family at the time of farewell.

Normadeene and the four children in front
of the White House in Washington D.C on
the way to New York.

The Gibson's first view of the US Capitol
building on the way to New York.

G.A. and Gibby in front of the
Pan Am Terminal

Chapter IV

ENGLAND, FRANCE AND SWITZERLAND

We found out immediately why it is important to travel lightly as far as luggage is concerned. In hopes of saving money, we tried to get by with only one taxi. However, due to the small size of the taxi cabs, and the six of us with our luggage, that was impossible, as even two cabs were barely enough to accommodate us. We had booked into The Mount Royal Hotel on Oxford Street in downtown London. We believe the cab driver took us there by the shortest possible route, as he seemed to be very sympathetic with our plight, as well as the late hour.

After checking into the Mount Royal Hotel we walked across the street to The Golden Egg Restaurant where we enjoyed an early morning breakfast of fish and chips. We wondered why everybody seemed to be watching us. I guess it was a strange sight to see a family of six eating out so early in the morning. The children seemed to be enjoying it though, as they stared right back at their English friends.

One of the reasons we decided to travel to Africa by way of Europe was for the educational opportunity it would afford the children. We planned to take in all of the sights we had heard so much about and read about. We had just watched the movie Mary Poppins and were excited about seeing St. Paul's Cathedral where the famous *feed the birds* scene took place. We had

read about The Tower of London and Westminster
Abbey, so filled with British History. Also, we were
anxious to see The Changing of the Guard at
Buckingham Palace as well as Number Ten Downing
Street made famous as the headquarters of Winston
Churchill during the Second World War. I was
especially interested in spending some time in The
British Museum, as it held many of the treasures of
archaeology I had lectured about in my college class
room. It harbored one of the oldest existing
manuscripts of the Old Testament, as well as the Code
of Hammurabi believed to believe the oldest code of
law in existence.

We visited all of these places and took many
pictures and made recordings on our little tape
recorder of everything we found of interest. Some
day I will take the time to listen to those recordings,
as I recorded something every day from the time we
left Minnesota until we arrived back home

We found that time went by far too rapidly and it
was soon time to get packed and fly off to Orly
Airport in Paris, France. However, we were able to
do one more thing that I had often dreamed of. We
were within walking distance of Hyde Park. We
took in a dog show that proved to be fascinating
as it featured English Sheep Dogs who were
remarkable in their ability to obey commands. But
more important to me was Oratory Corner where
people from all over the world, from all walks of
life, were free to stand up on a wooden box and
expound on whatever subject prompted them. I found
myself, much to the embarrassment of my family,
standing on a box expounding the Gospel of Jesus
Christ and answering questions about our mission
to Ghana, West Africa.

Normadeene and I have never been back to

London, however, several of our children have
revisited there and had many pleasant experiences
recalled to their memory. We plan to retrace our
steps some day, too.

We flew across the English Channel and landed
at Orly Field near Paris. It took only a few minutes
to fly from London to Paris. This time we called for
two taxi cabs to take us to The Madelin Palace Hotel.
It was located just a stone's throw from the famous
Paris Opera House and also the American Express
offices.

Unlike our arrival in England, we arrived in Paris
around noon. As usual, the first thing we heard from
the children was, "We're hungry!" Our hotel room
was beautiful. It was furnished with antiques and
had thick carpets. The walls were decorated with
lovely paintings. The beds were feather beds in which
you would sink out of sight as the folds of the blankets
completely enveloped your body. The Mount Royal
was nice, but this was elegant! We were not used to
this kind of accommodations. We loved it.

As we mentioned, the children were hungry,
so we set out to find a place to eat. I had
instructed the children to attempt to order
moderately priced meals as our budget was rather
limited. I have not been allowed to forget how I
attempted to impress the elevator operator with
my French. Somehow I managed to say, "Si Si",
rather than "Oui Oui."

There was a very nice restaurant on the lower
level of our hotel. Normadeene and I wanted to find
a pretty little Sidewalk Cafe, but the children were
too hungry to wait, so we decided to eat there. We
were met by the Maitre' d. who seated us at a table
with a clean white linen table cloth and beautiful
silverware and crystal settings. He was the only one

who could speak English, so he took our orders. Little did we realize how we were being watched and how the things we did affected those around us. It is so true that "We are writing a gospel a chapter a day, by the deeds that we do and the words that we say. Man reads what you write, whether faithless or true. What is the gospel according to you?" Or in other words, very few people read the Four Gospels. They read the Fifth Gospel, our lives. I mentioned this, because it was, and still is our habit to offer a prayer of thanksgiving to God before every meal. So after the Maitre' d. left, we bowed our heads and offered thanks to our Lord for the blessings he had already bestowed upon us in bringing us safely to Paris, and also for the blessing of the meal we were about to receive. Before we finished our prayer we heard a chair move and footsteps coming towards us. We looked up to see a man rushing to our table with his hand stretched out crying In a loud voice, "Thank you! Thank you! Thank you! Thank you for praying as a family. I am from New York and it has been so long since I have heard a family pray. That was so wonderful. Thank you for praying that prayer!" Isn't it interesting that a business man from New York found a simple thing like a prayer before a meal, which we take for granted, so special to him. That experience has repeated itself often through the years since that moment in Paris.

After eating, we decided to take a bus tour of Paris, and then later go on our own to see the sights we most desired to see. We believe that was a good idea and would recommend that to those who have only a short time to spend in Paris.

The Eiffel Tower stood out like a sentinel towering over Paris. You could see it wherever you went. The children managed to climb to the top. We just watched, as we did not have the energy to follow them

Our bus tour took us by The Are de Triumph, past the Notre Dame Cathedral with its famous Gargoyles. We imagined seeing Charles Laughton, the Hunch Back, looking down from the bell tower. It also took us by the Louvre Museum which was one of my main points of interest, as was the case with the British Museum. Soon after we embarked on our quest to see the sights of Paris on our own, I noticed a man following us. G.A. and I had become separated from the rest of the family, and as we walked by a doorway, the man rushed up to us and asked if we had any money we wanted to exchange. He offered us a rate that was far more generous than the legal rate at the currency exchange. The Lord knows we could use every dollar we could possibly save. But as tempting as it was, I decided that as guests in the beautiful city of Paris, we would not take advantage of the situation, and violate the conditions upon which we were afforded the hospitality of France. The man was hard to convince, but he finally gave up on me and left us to find someone else to offer such a good deal. I have always had a good feeling about overcoming that temptation, and I know that G. A. was proud of the example his father set for him that day in Paris.

The time we spent in the Louvre was the most memorable of all of the places we visited on our way to Africa. Seeing the paintings of the Masters with our own eyes made a lasting impression on us. We received special permission to take some pictures of paintings such as the Mona Lisa and Whistlers Mother. I explained how I was going to establish a college in Africa and that many of my students would never be able to travel to Paris. However, I could show them the pictures they allowed me to take. That was in 1966. Today that would not be possible, and for good reasons, Today I have a poster picture of the Mona Lisa hanging on the wall of our living room. Fond memories flood our hearts every time we look at it.

There was a cafe in the basement of the Louvre. That was good, as there was no way one could begin to view all of the art treasures in less than a few days. That made it very convenient. I recall there was a porch up the marble staircase past Winged Victory where there were chairs and tables where one could eat his lunch. Our family loaded up on food and headed up that marble staircase past Winged Victory. Half way up the stairs, past Winged Victory, G.A.'s chicken slipped off of his plate. I will never forget the sight of seeing that chicken breast tumble down those marble stairs past winged victory.

As was the case with London, so it was with Paris. The time went by far too fast. However, it was time to pack up and head for Geneva, Switzerland. As mentioned earlier we are anxious to retrace our tracks through Paris before we leave this planet. It wasn't easy to take four children to Paris, but to this day they will tell you it was one of the most meaningful experiences of their lives. It was well worth any sacrifice.

We flew from Paris to Geneva, Switzerland. There we stayed in the Beau Ravage Hotel which overlooked beautiful Lake Geneva with its giant water spout sending plumes of water into the sky like Yellowstone's Old Faithful.

By now we were starting to get butter flies in our stomachs again, as we realized we would soon be leaving Switzerland to fly to Ghana. We had only a few more days to spend here and we wanted to make the most of them. However, try as we may, we could never completely get rid of those butter flies, and the thought we would soon be leaving for Ghana.

Switzerland was beautiful! Words fail to describe the splendor of its towering mountain peaks. It reminded us so much of some of the scenery we have in the Rocky Mountains. However, somehow at the time, the Alps seemed much more stark and treacherous to us. We can never remove the image of the Matterhorn's majestic peak from our minds, as its snowy peak glistened in the sun light.

There was so much we desired to see in Switzerland and we were only there for a short time, so we decided to tour the country via the railroad. We booked passage on a cable car train which was powered by electricity We left Geneva and traveled north toward Montrose and Gestadt. The scenery was breath taking. The country side was decked with flowers and the Swiss Chalets almost looked unreal as they dotted the countryside with their bright colors and immaculatly clean look.

Unfortunately, all did not go well on our trip through the Alps. Cindy became ill and vomited all over herself However, a kind and resourceful conductor helped her to clean up, and she fared well the rest of the trip. We had delicious Swiss steak in Gestadt, in fact it was the best I had ever tasted. And that is quite a complement because Normadeene is an excellent cook and has made delicious Swiss steak often.

I believe I should mention that it was Sunday when we took our trip by rail through the Alps. One of the most memorable things we did while traveling through England, France and Switzerland, were the times we shared devotions together, and more specifically the times we shared The Lord's Supper in our hotel room. We never missed having communion together on The Lord's Day from the time we left Minnesota until we arrived back home from Ghana. It was a very special time because it bonded us with our friends back in America, as we knew they too were observing the Lord's Supper, perhaps at the same time as we.

We arrived back in our hotel late Sunday evening, upon which time we immediately began to pack our things to get ready to fly to Ghana via Swiss Air the next morning. We arranged for a shuttle bus to take us to the airport. It was waiting for us the next morning and took us to the terminal. The butter flies in our stomachs were now bigger than ever. We were about to fly over Southern Switzerland, Italy, the Mediterranean Sea, The Sahara Desert and North Africa to our destination in Ghana, West Africa. Our long waited for, and prayed for, adventure was about to begin. Little did we know what was in store for us. However, even though we did not know what the future held for us, we did know Who holds the future. We knew that God had placed His angels in charge over us. Psalms 91:11 We also knew it would be well worth any sacrifice we might have to make.

Our Swiss Air jet made landings at Roberts Field in Liberia, Dakar, Senegal, and Lagos Nigeria before it finally circled International Airport in Accra, Ghana West Africa. It made a soft landing. The heat was stifling as we were right on the equator, approximately zero longitude and zero latitude. We were in Ghana at last!

Jerry Gibson in front of the British
Museum

Normadeene and Becky in front of Number
Ten Downing St in London

Normadeene and the children in front
of the Airport in Paris, France

Chapter V

TIIE BANK DRAFT ANGEL

Our jet taxied toward the air terminal. We were about to begin the adventure of our lives. Many thoughts flooded our minds. What would it be like to go through customs? We had heard many horror stories about how difficult that would be. What would it cost us to bring our unaccompanied baggage into Ghana? What about our health certificates, would they be in order? What about money, would we be able to get American dollars exchanged for the currency of Ghana? Who would be there to meet us and act as our interpreters? We did not know a word of the language of Ghana. We were not sure about our Visas. It took us almost nine months to get them approved, and they were only temporary. We knew our passports were in order, as we had little difficulty going through Europe. We were told to never let them out of our sight, as they were more valuable than all of the money we brought with us

When our airplane came to a stop, the flight attendant opened the door and a rush of hot, humid air filled the plane. It brought with it an odor that never left us from the time we deplaned that aircraft, until we boarded the Pan Am jet that would take us back to America some months later. It was the smell of a mixture of burned charcoal and salt water mixed with the smell of stale flowers

A Ghana Airways shuttle bus pulled up to the side of our plane. It stopped some distance from the terminal. I wondered why it stopped so far out. It was painted with the national colors of Ghana, yellow and green with the large black star of Ghana painted on its side. Another shuttle pulled along side to take our baggage into the Terminal. We were hot and tired, and wondered if we would ever see those who had come to meet us. Then the thought occurred to us once again, who if anybody will be here to meet us, and how long have they been waiting? About that time we heard the sound of African drums and singing and dancing. An African man moved toward us through the crowded terminal and introduced himself as Brother Sampong from Afrancho. He said he recognized us from a picture we had sent. He, along with twenty other men and women, had traveled some three hundred miles from the Ashanti Territory to greet us. When Normadeene and the children were cleared by the health authorities, they were allowed to accompany Brother Sampong outside the terminal building to meet their new friends. We had carefully prepared speeches to make, but somehow none of them seemed appropriate at that time. It was the middle of the night and we were very tired and already suffering from cultural shock. Normadeene asked, "What shall we do?" Brother Sampong spoke very broken English, and we spoke no Ghanaian. I said, "Just stand there and look at them and smile."

As I was going through customs, I could hear the Africans singing and dancing to the sound of the drum beat, and I could picture in my mind Normadeene and the children standing there and just smiling.

Getting through customs was not easy. I was handed six forms for each member of our family to fill out. It was almost like writing an autobiography of each of us. They wanted to know everything about us, and about everything we desired to bring into Ghana with us, as well as what unaccompanied baggage would follow. I had to declare the value of our cameras, watches and other jewelry as well as the amount of cash money we were bringing into the country. Because of what they called *foreign exchange* we would not be allowed to take any more American money out of the country than what we brought in

One of the questions they asked was destined to produce what we may call *a comedy of errors.* They asked if we brought any firearms or ammunition with us? You may recall that Dean Howard Hayes of Minnesota Bible College talked me into buying a little twenty-two pistol for killing snakes, spiders or rats. I did not know that firearms of any kind were forbidden in Ghana. Not even the policemen were allowed to carry firearms Only the military was allowed to do so. As honest as I was, I declared my pistol and ammunition. Unfortunately, that was not the end of the story, which you will hear about later and gain many a chuckle over. I also declared every dollar we were bringing into the country. I thought we would have enough money with us to last until we were settled some place. Then I would contact our forwarding agent to set up a bank account for us in one of the banks in Ghana. However, I was in for the shock of my life. Customs took almost every cent we had. They left us with only enough money for one nights lodging in Accra, and transportation to Kumasi the next day, and enough money for one nights lodging there, and breakfast the next morning. We were in deep trouble! Where was our Guardian Angel now, when we needed him the most, so far away from home in a strange land? A panic attack hit my stomach. How was I to tell Normadeene and the Children that we were broke? The worst part of it all was, nobody at home knew where we were. As I suggested earlier, we thought we had enough money to last us at least a month after arriving in Ghana. That would give us the time to locate and establish a permanent address, and also establish a bank account. We would then make arrangements for our forwarding agent to contact our bank in Havre, Montana to transfer funds from our account in Havre to the bank in Ghana whenever needed. However, things did not work out that way for us. Being in a strange country with your wife and four children, without any money, not knowing where you are, and not being able to speak the language is a frightening situation. Once again I remind the reader that if you can keep your composure, when all around you are losing theirs, most likely you don't understand the situation!

Brother Sampong informed us that we would stay over night in Accra and leave early the next morning for Kumasi, the capitol of the Ashanti Territory. Some referred to Kumasi as *the place of human sacrifice,* a term we would later understand. I would rather refer to Kumasi as *The Garden City,* as it proved to be just that. We did not know why The Universal Christian Church wanted us to headquarter in Kumasi, but we trusted the Lord was leading, and later found out that the majority of the leaders who called us to Ghana were from that part of Ghana. They wanted us to establish the college there.

We found a small cottage near Flagstaff House to stay that first night. Normadeene informed me later that when she pulled back the sheets, a huge, black Hercules beetle came running out from under my covers. They have ugly looking sharp pinchers, and can leave a nasty bite. She knew I would have never gone to sleep had she told me about that ugly bug. In spite of the fact I did not know about the *monster* in our bed, at the best I had a fitful steep. I kept wondering how we were going to survive without any money, and more urgent, how was I to inform Normadeene and the children of our dilemma?

Early the next morning we were greeted by the people from Afrancho who had traveled so far to take care of us. The African people use the rising and setting of the sun to determine their rising and retiring for the day. That was their *nature's alarm clock. It s*eemed earlier than it actually was because we were still exhausted from the events of the day before. It continued to be very hot and humid, which also contributed to our difficult time sleeping.

We boarded a *Mammy Wagon* that was supposed to seat twelve people at the *most*. However, including the six in our family, there were thirty of us jammed into that little vehicle! We were now in for another *cultural shock!* There were no nice clean rest rooms or convenience stations we refer to as rest stops. There was about two-hundred and seventy-five miles of almost impassible roads through dense jungle, over mountains and rickety bridges crossing the many rivers and streams. When people needed a *comfort stop* they informed the driver, who would then pull over to the side of the road. The people who needed to relieve themselves would pile out, and proceed to do what they had to do, in plain view, right there on the side of the road. Words can not describe the shocked looks on the faces of our Children, as they experienced this for the first time, They soon got used to it as it was just a part of the Ghanain way of life when traveling.

We arrived in Kumasi late that afternoon. I

informed our African friends that we were very short on cash. They found us a place to stay that first night in a very low income part of Kumasi. It was the La Rosa Hotel. We had just enough money for one night of lodging, and breakfast the next morning. As we contemplate this experience, we can still smell the smells of burned charcoal and see the vulture covered garbage dump, as well as a public toilet, all located very close to our hotel. We had scrambled eggs and coca cola for breakfast. We were surprised to find, wherever we traveled, signs advertising "Drink Coca Cola." even in the densest part of the jungle. The church might do well to learn something from "the people of the world" in this respect.

After we finished what I thought may prove to be our *last breakfast,* as we were now completely broke, the man who prepared and served us our breakfast, decided to take his morning bath. He stripped down to his *birthday suit* in front of us. That was the second big culture shock experienced within our first twenty-four hours in Africa. He then decided to wash his clothing. He washed his clothing in the same water he had used for his bath! He then decided to wash the dishes from which we had just eaten. He used the same water he had used for his bath and washing his clothing!

Normadeene lost it! She ran into the little hut of a room we had all slept in the night before. She sobbed, "I don't believe I can take it! I don't believe I can stay in Africa!" I had informed her of our financial predicament, and that, along with the fact that when we entered our hut in the La Rosa Hotel, we were greeted by a swarm of ants carrying a dead lizard up the wall right beside the mattress where we slept on the floor the night before. All of that, and the thought of our host's lack of hygiene, seemed too much at the time for her to bear. At a time like that, like the fact that it has been claimed t*here are no atheists in a fox hole,* all we could do was turn to God and remind Him of His promise that *He would give His angels charge over us.* We got on our knees and prayed to our God. I assured Normadeene that God never gives His people a task to perform without providing the means to accomplish that task. We continued to do some very serious praying

While we were praying, the thought came to me that we should walk down town in Kumasi and find a bank. We would have to walk, as we did not have taxi fare. We would then ask the bank to wire our bank in Havre for money.

When we arrived down town, after walking through the fascinating Kumasi market place, where one could buy almost anything you can imagine, we found there were three banks from which to choose. There was the Bank of Ghana, the Bank of West Africa and the Barclay Bank. We chose the Barclay Bank because of its pretty blue and white color. My high school colors were blue and white. "Blue white, blue white, we do do fight!" we used to chant. Anything that reminded us of home was a comfort at the time. We walked up the steps into the bank. As we entered the bank, a voice came over the P.A. system, "Is there a Professor Gibson in the bank?" We were in a state of shock, Nobody knew we were in Kumasi! We did not know where we would be settling, and were going to wait until we had an address, etc., before informing our forwarding agent. The people in Havre had no idea where we were at the time all of this was happening. The voice on the P.A. system continued on and said, "If you are in the bank, please come to the office." We walked down the hall and opened the door to the office. There sat a bespectacled, dignified looking Englishman. He asked to see our passports. He then told us that a man had just left a bank draft for one thousand dollars for us. He said the man was gone before he could obtain any information from him. He told us to sign a paper. We did, and walked out into the lobby with a bank draft for one thousand dollars in our hands. We opened a bank account and left the bank. To this day nobody has a clue as to where that money came from. That is, nobody but us. We are certain that it came from God, and our angel left it there.

Map of the Continent of Africa

Flagstaff House,
Ghana's Military Headquarters

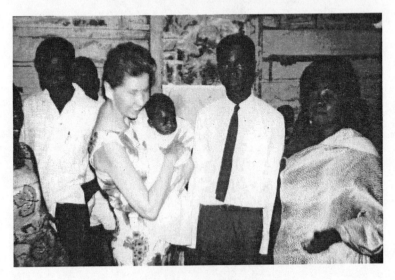

Normadeene with pastor Hayford and wife
with the baby named after her.

Normadeene and Becky
with Pastor Mensah's wife in Kumasi

Chapter VI

ANGELS IN THE NIGHT

We were able to find a suitable place to live and conduct classes just outside of Kumasi across from the little village of Susonsu. It was on the Accra road and was owned by a barrister's wife, Mrs. Adun. She and her children lived in one half of the two story duplex like building, and our family and the college occupied the other half. Our automobile and other personal effects had not yet arrived from America. We had to have bunk beds with straw mattresses, a table and several chairs made by a local carpenter. We were able to purchase one knife, fork and spoon, and also one dish, bowl, cup and a couple of plastic glasses at the market place. The market place, as suggested earlier, was an adventure in itself. There were row upon row of vendors, mostly Ghanaian women, selling everything imaginable. If you had the money, one could buy anything from penicillin to lace table cloths. At that time, one American dollar would not buy a Ghanaian cedi. Today, one U.S. dollar is worth close to five-hundred cedi. That tells the tragic story of the economic dilemma Ghana has faced since receiving its independence. We were far enough out from Kumasi that we had to depend upon taxis for transportation. You had to *haggle* with the taxi driver in regard to the fare. This was true with any business dealings you might have in the market place, also.

We had a place to conduct classes. Now, we had to find a student body. Two of the young men who had come to meet us in Accra lived with us, and were very valuable, as they helped us conduct business, and also acted as our guides and interpreters. One of them was Isaac Gyedu, who attended Ghana Christian College, who today is a prominent evangelist in West Africa. The other was Benjamin Amanqua, who also attended the college.

Isaac and Benjamin arranged for me to speak in the square, under the Mango trees, in Ahanti New Town. That was just about a block from the palace of the Ashanti Hene, the most powerful king and paramount chief in the Ashanti Territory, of which Kumasi was the capital. We positioned ourselves in a prominent place, and then Isaac and Benjamin started to beat on their drums. It was not long before a large crowd of all ages had gathered to hear what the strange "Obroni," which is the Ghanaian name for a white man, had to say. As I recall, I preached on the subject "Dare to be a Daniel". I explained that we had come to Ghana to establish a college for training African evangelists and ministers of the Gospel. I then gave an invitation for specialized Christian servants who would become the first students of Ghana Christian College and Seminary. Twelve young men responded to God's call that night. I was called back to Ghana in 1991 to be the keynote speaker for the college's Silver Anniversary. Today there are close to seven hundred graduates preaching all over Africa. Rockeybell Adatura, the number one evangelist among Muslims in West Africa, is one of the graduates from Ghana Christian College and Seminary.

We had to take a cab back to Susonsu. That meant driving through the Muslim district of Kumasi. The Muslims, for the most part, had very little love for Christians, and less love for a white Christian mssionary. I can still smell the charcoal pots and hear the sounds as we made our way through that section of Ashanti New Town. I could feel the hair standing up on my neck, but my fears were soon dispelled, as I knew my Angel was watching over me. Never the less, I felt a sigh of relief as we pulled up to our home.

I was very excited about the twelve young men who had responded to the call to become the first students of Ghana Christian College. I ran upstairs to tell Normadeene the good news. Just about then, we heard a scream. It was the kind of scream you never want to hear at any time or any place. However, you especially did not want to hear it in Africa at a time when we had no means of transportation, and were not familiar with any kind of aid in times of an emergency. We recognized that scream as coming from our youngest son, G.A.

We ran down stairs and started to scold G.A. and the rest of the children for not minding us, as we had asked them not to tear around, as we were afraid they might get hurt. Isaac and Benjamin had boiled a large pan of water in order to wash the dishes.Somehow, G.A. had backed into that pan of scalding water and sat down in it! We realized how badly he was hurt when he cried, "Daddy, don't yell at me! Pray for me!" Coming from our twelve year old son, who was not interested in much more than G.I. Joe and James Bond, we knew that we were in deep trouble.

Our situation seemed impossible. We were living several miles outside of Kumasi on the Accra road.

After sundown, very few vehicles ventured out that way. There was a Technical Training College a few miles down the road, but it was closed down during the weekend. The likelihood of anybody being out there or being on that road at that time on a Sunday night was very small. I ran out of the house into the middle of the road. It was pitch black, as there is no twilight in that part of Africa. It was like pulling down the shades, and it was dark time. I stood there listening to the screams of our little boy who was in much pain, and prayed for help! Just then, headlights appeared down the road. A taxi pulled up out of the darkness. The driver inquired, "Do you need help?" That same question was asked of Becky and me years later on top of Vale Mountain when we found ourselves freezing to death, bogged down in snow up to our arm pits. Out of nowhere a man appeared and asked, "Do you need help?" He led us to safety and then was gone. We explained our situation, and then carried G.A. out to the cab and placed him in a position with his face down, because the pain was unbearable if he sat down.

It suddenly dawned on us, as the cab pulled away, that the driver had not asked us to pay the fare, that once again, God sent His angel to help us in our hour of grave need. The *angel driver* took us to the City Hospital in Kumasi. It was a place were the only people brought there, usually came to die. Large Turkey Vultures lurked all around the grounds of the hospital, adding to the feeling if despair one had when forced into such a situation as we were experiencing. It seemed like a terrible nightmare, but that was only wishful thinking. G. A. sobbed and moaned from his awkward position all of the way to the hospital. His pain was excruciating, and we wish we could have borne it for him. It was a

very painful situation for us too, but a different kind
of pain. The kind of pain that a mother and father
feel when they have to stand helplessly by. All we
could do is trust in the promises of God that He
would not allow us to suffer what we were not
able to bear, and He would provide a way out of
our dilemma. I Corinthians 10:13. We were about
to experience the longest night of our lives.
However, we found comfort from the words of the
Psalmist, "Weeping may endure at night, but joy
comes in the morning!" Psalms 30:5.

Jerry in front of Mammy Wagon

Chapter VII

THE LONGEST NIGHT

We were met by a nurse receptionist, who informed us there was no doctor available. The hospital had only one doctor to serve a community of over 250 thousand people We found out later that he was from China and had only a minimal medical school education from an Iron Curtain country. The nurse looked at G.A.'s injury and gasped, "There is nothing we can do for him until the doctor gets back!" When we first examined G.A., I tried to remove his shorts, but flesh was stuck to the cloth and came off of his little groin, as I tried to remove them. The nurse scribbled a prescription on a small piece of paper and said, "Get this filled and bring back the first thing tomorrow morning." We were then given a wheelchair for G.A. and sent up to the fourth floor of the hospital to the place where kings and chiefs came to die. The Bantama Hene was there waiting to die. I had prayer with him several times before he passed away. The most difficult moment for us was when we were told we could not stay with him that night. We had to walk out of that ward to the elevator, and leave G.A. alone in such terrible pain. We were told that he would most likely have to have his legs amputated. Infection spreads so rapidly in that part of Africa, and that may be necessary to save his life. With that thought, not knowing whether we would see our son alive again, we had to take, what to us, was the longest walk of our lives, out of that hospital to the traffic circle where we would have to find a way back to Susonsu. We also had the added concern as to where we would find a pharmacy to fill the prescription, and get it back to the hospital early the next morning. I knew that Normadeene could not stand much more of this and was about to her breaking point. We needed help immediately! It was time for urgent prayer. We needed help from our angel who had always been there for us before. I started to pray like I had never prayed before. It was midnight. We did not know where we were, or how to get back home. The possibility of anybody in a vehicle, or a taxi cab being out at that time of night was very small. It was at the beginning of *the rainy season.* It rained as much as two-hundred inches in one month. It started to rain. We were desperate! I continued to pray for help.

Just then, out of the darkness and the rain, we heard a voice calling, "Professor Gibson, It is I, Nicholas! It is I, Nicholas! Don't you remember me? It is I, Nicholas!" We had befriended a taxi driver earlier that week. Little did we realize that he would prove to be an angel, as proclaimed in Hebrews 13:2. "Do not forget to entertain strangers, for by so doing, you have unwittingly entertained angels." We asked him what he was doing there at that late hour. He said he really did not know, but felt an urging at his heart and was somehow led to our location. We told him of our need. We especially impressed upon him the urgency of getting the prescription filled and back to the hospital early the next morning. He said as he dropped us off at our home, he would be back for us early in the morning.

We slept very little that night. G.A. was on our minds, and we prayed for him all night long. When we finally dozed off, we woke to the sound of a taxi-cab horn, and the loud calling, "It is I Nicholas! It is I, Nicholas! I have come to take you to the pharmacy and back to the hospital." As long as we live, there will probably never be sweeter words to our ears, than the words we heard that night on the traffic circle by the hospital, and the words we heard again that morning, "It is I, Nicholas!"

Our *angel taxi driver,* Nicholas, drove us to a part of Kumasi we had not been before. The streets were very narrow, lined with places of business very close to each other. He pulled up to a building that had a sign marked *Pharmacy.* Nicholas took the prescription in his hand and started pounding on a door that was hinged at the middle. Pretty soon the top part of the door swung open, and there stood a little gray haired African lady. Nicholas handed her the piece of paper with the prescription, and proceeded to impress upon her in the Akan language, the urgency of our getting that prescription filled and back to the hospital. She scanned with her eyes a wall covered with little cubby holes, each one marked with a code number which only she understood. She spotted the one she was looking for, and reached and pulled out a dusty tube, the last one there. She handed it to Nicholas. Once again, God had provided for our need.

The prescription in the tube contained an anti-biotic ointment that was supposed to both soothe the pain and also help prevent infection. As suggested earlier, infection spreads very rapidly in that hot, damp climate. The only way G.A. could stand the pain when they rubbed the ointment over his burns, was for me to grip his hand tightly, and pray and read scriptures. It was very embarrassing for him, as his burns were in his privates, and he was at a stage in his life when he was very modest. Most of the African nurses had never seen a naked white boy before, and to G.A.'s discomfort, they giggled as they applied the ointment to his body.

While Normadeene stood there feeling helpless, watching the nurses apply the ointmnet, an old African man came to her side, sensing the turmoil and pain she was experiencing, he placed his hand on her shoulder and softly whispered in her ear, "Mama, God can take our bad times and turn them into good times." A complete sense of peace enveloped Normadeene's heart. At that moment she knew that all would be well with our son.

As mentioned earlier, it was suggested that they may have to amputate G.A.'s legs. That was not necessary. When we came back the next morning we were called over to G.A.'s bedside. The nurses excitedly proclaimed to us, "There has been a miracle! Your son is completely healed!" I was not willing to sacrifice my son like Abraham. God did not place that temptation in our way. There was not even a scar to show where he had been burned! When we shared this good news with our twelve students, they said, "We already knew that." We asked them, "How?" They replied, "We have been praying for him and for you," in a *matter of fact* tone of voice.

The little old man was right. God can take our bad times and turn them into good times. From that day on the hospital staff conducted prayer meetings every morning. God demonstrated in a powerful way that "He causes *all things* to work together for good for those who love Him, and are called according to His purpose."

Another thing that happened at that time, that blessed us so much, and continues to bless us, was the fact that when my sister Harriet Lufrano and her husband Tony heard about G.A.'s injury, they sent us a wire and told us not to worry about any costs that might incur. They went on to say that they would cover all medical and hospital expenses, even if it required their selling everything they owned. That kind of love is very precious and very rare, even among families. We have often commented that *It is possible to give without loving, but it is impossible to love without giving.* Harriet and Tony Lufrano expressed that kind of love for us.

We were concerned about how we would pay for G.A.'s doctor bills and hospital bills. However when we checked out of the hospital, the only charges we owed were for medications. All other expenses were covered by the government of Ghana.

God took such good care of us. From that time forth, we no longer had the *"spirit of fear, but of power, love and self-control."* II Timothy 1:7

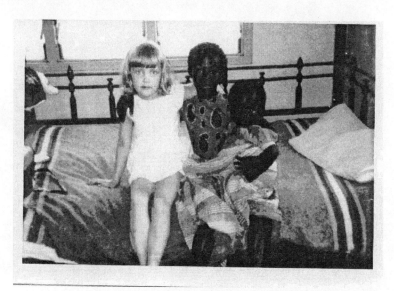

Becky with two of her African friends
in our home in Kumasi

Gibby with Mrs. Adun's children in front of
our home in Kumasi

Chapter VIII

AFRANCHO AND CHIEF MENSAH

Soon after our experience with G.A., I traveled with Benjamin and Isaac to the little town of Afrancho, where most of those who met us at the airport in Accra lived. Before we left the States for Africa, Normadeene had a strange dream about a village in Ghana where the soil was a bright rusty red. When we approached Afrancho I immediately thought about her dream, as the soil and color of the dirt streets were exactly as she had described them to be so many months earlier in our motel in Minneapolis. It gave me a strange feeling. When she returned with me to Afrancho some time later, she affirmed the fact that her dream described that little village.

Before saying any more, I would like to mention that as we drove out of Kumasi toward Afrancho, I noticed back off of the right side of the road a strange brick building covered with vines and underbrush. At the entrance were two monumental lions with an African standing guard. I wondered what it was and my curiosity gained strength as we drove away. From that time on, whenever we drove out of Kumasi in that direction, my curiosity was revived. I will say more about this later on, as you are probably curious too, by now. I will tell you now that it was a *mausoleum.*

My first night in Afrancho was a difficult one. Upon arriving in Afrancho, I was taken to a two storied house that was only about half finished. I was led upstairs where there was a small room with window openings, but no glass or screens. There was a plain, bare little table in the middle of the room, and one little wooden chair by the table. Just off of that room, there was another little room with no windows and no means of lighting. In that room there was a wooden platform, and on the platform was an old, dirty, wet smelly mattress. It was the bed I was to sleep on that night!

A big man with a shiny bald head led the host of elders from the Afrancho Church who were there to meet me. Brother Sampong, the pastor of their church, had sent them to welcome me, and to see that I had the things I needed and was comfortable. I assured them that all was well, and after praying with them, they left me there by myself. But before long, they were back in force, all of them. They had brought me my supper. It consisted of a plate of rice mixed with some kind of red meat. I immediately noticed that some little black bugs were crawling around in my supper. We had been told by other missionaries that it would be considered an insult to not eat the food that was placed before us. That proved to be one of the many *myths* in regard to life as a missionary in Africa. The Africans wanted us to be honest with them about everything, just as we desired the same from them. However, I might add, one must be kind and tactful when doing so. One should be *lovingly* honest.

Normadeene gave me a peanut butter sandwich and a bottle of water to take with me in case I needed them. That proved to be *my salvation* and a stroke of genius. I would take a bite of the food that had been placed before me, and then a bite of the peanut butter sandwich. I would then wash them down with the water in the bottle. It was not safe for us to drink the water from the village, so it was standard practice to carry boiled water with us at all times.

The men of Afrancho watched every bite I took. Finally, I ate all I could, so I announced that I was full. To my dismay, all of them immediately scrambled to finish off what was left on my plate. I learned later that they had given me the food they would have eaten that evening. I felt very humble, and half way ashamed for not appreciating it more at the time. Today I do appreciate their sacrificial sharing with me.

There was no electricity in that unfinished building, so when the sun went down I was to go to bed. But first, they told that me some women from the village were coming to give me my bath. That brought a feeling of panic and terror into my heart! I was not about to have some strange, half naked African women give me a bath. The women of that village are not always as fully dressed as are our women in America. At least that used to be so. Because of the extreme heat, they often did not wear anything on the upper part of their bodies. Bare breasts were common in African villages, but they had not yet become common to me. Because of my cultural background and code of modesty, they never have become common. I quickly assured them that I had bathed just before leaving Kumasi, and therefore did not need or desire another bath. With some reluctance, they agreed to forego the bath. I later learned that the Africans think that Europeans, which all white people are considered to be, stink. Not being willing to let them give me a bath further supported their theory.

That night, in that little, dark, damp room, sleeping on that dirty, wet smelly mattress, with no windows for ventilation, and no means of lighting, was one of the longest nights I have ever experienced. I could feel strange creatures crawling over my body all night long, but could not see them. I could only hope and pray they would not bite or sting me. God heard my prayers, as I finally managed to doze off into a troubled sleep, and woke up the next morning to the calling of the elders telling me they had brought me my breakfast. It was the same as they had brought for my supper the night before. I decided to declare to them that I was fasting. This tactic saved me many times since then. They said they understood, and as before, they proceeded to devour every bit of what was on that plate.

The order of the business of that day, which was Sunday, was to first go to the Afrancho Church. I was to deliver the morning message, after which I was to accompany the pastor and elders to the palace of Chief Mensah. I was to be given an audience with him. This was a great honor. The worship service in the Afrancho Church was one I will long remember. The music was accompanied by the playing of drums. I had never witnessed such an exciting, joy filled congregation of people! They sang like a choir of a thousand angels. When it came time for the morning offering, the women, dressed in beautiful colored Manchester cloth dresses, stood up and started to dance and sing toward a large wash basin that was placed in the front of the sanctuary to receive the offering. They waved their gaily colored handkerchiefs and sang, "Ya dawasi, Nyami, gwamba, Yeyiwo aye, Nyami gwamba, Ye kumfo wo, Nyami gwamba, Ya dawasi, Nyami gwamba!" This was in the *Twi* tongue and may be translated, "We thank thee O' Lord. We praise thee O' Lord. We glorify thee O' Lord. We thank thee O' Lord! After the women had all filed out, then the men joined them in their dance before the Lord. They danced around the big offering container and dropped in their offering as they passed by. After all had dropped in their offering, they quickly counted the money.If there was not as much as they thought it should be, they would start all over again, and dance around the offering pot until there was enough. At the close of this part of the service, they called for people, who thought they had been specially blessed that past week, to come forward and give a testimony, for the benefit of all who were present. They then presented a special magnanimous offering of thanks to the Lord. What I witnessed that morning was in sharp contrast to most of the services I was used to attending back in America. I wondered how the people in our churches would react to such freedom and open expression of love and adoration for God that was experienced by the Christians in Afrancho that morning.

I brought a message that morning entitled *Sign Posts of Sonship* from the second chapter of First John. Pastor Sampong insisted on being my interpreter. I warned him that I speak rather rapidly. Some one timed me one time and said that I spoke one-hundred words a minute, with gusts up to three-hundred. I told him my message would be rather lengthy due to having to speak through an interpreter. He assured me that he was up to the occasion. When I finished preaching, he had to find a place to lie down. All in all, it was a very joyous experience.

As I look back, one of the highlights of that service was the host of pregnant Ghanaian women who came forward at the close of the service for me to lay hands on their stomachs and pray they would deliver healthy babies. After meeting with Chief Mensah, I understood why they did so. Some months later I returned to Afrancho with Normadeene and the children. After I had preached, several of the ladies, whose stomachs I had laid my hands on and prayed, brought healthy babies to me and proudly placed them in my arms, thanking God for hearing my prayers on their behalf. They named many of them after our children.

I was then taken to be received by Chief Mensah. We walked into the *throne room* and there he was seated on his *chiefton stool*. Protocol demanded that he speak to me through an interpreter who stood by his side holding a golden linguist staff. Before any further business could be conducted, I had to drink from the *mina-min-so, the drink for the weary traveler.* It consisted of a large calabash containing some kind of strange wine. I lost forty pounds of weight my first few months in Ghana from drinking *the drink for the weary traveler.* I found out later, while taking African Studies at The University of Ghana, that one could either drink out of the calabash, or pour it on the ground for the ancestors. From then on, I poured it on the ground for the ancestors and let them lose the weight.

Chief Mensah began by asking me, "What is your mission?" I responded by telling him that I had come to Ghana with my family to establish a Christian College for training African ministers and evangelists and teachers who could reach their own people with the gospel of Jesus Christ. He replied that there were a number of young men and women from his village who he desired to have attend Ghana Christian College. I repeated the words *Ghana Christian College* several times and asked if that didn't sound good to his ears?

He then touched my heart as he broke out into tears. He sobbed as he related the sad story that during the night a mother and child both died, as the mother attempted to bring the child into the world. He went on to explain to me how many others had died in child birth, and many had miscarriages. I now understood why the women had me lay hands on their stomachs and pray.

He begged me to help get somebody to set up a small clinic in his village to minister to the needs of the women and help them bring forth healthy babies. From that time on, every time I visited villages in that area, I found myself laying hands on the stomachs of women who had lost babies. The greatest honor an African woman could have was to bear a healthy child. That is in sharp contrast with our American society where *right to life* is being fought over in our courts.

I assured Chief Mensah I would do all in my power to get somebody to come to Ghana and establish the small clinic that was so much needed for his people. All that was needed was someone who could teach the basics of hygiene and prenatal care, and dispense prescription drugs. Such a person or persons would be of great value to the women in that area.

We prayed that God would send the right people to meet this need. God immediately answered our prayer in the persons of Edgar and Mable Nichols. Edgar had visited Ghana earlier and was acquainted with the situation there. He had many friends throughout the country. We had seen him in Omaha, Nebraska shortly before leaving for Ghana. Edgar and Mabel were both in their late sixties or early seventies when they agreed to respond to the call to

set up a clinic in Afrancho. We were confident that
what they lacked in physical stamina, due to their
age, would be more than compensated for by their
tremendous love for the Ghanaian people, along with
their strong sense of commitment and unwavering
faith in their mission. We eagerly looked forward to
the day Edgar and Mabel would arrive on the soil of
Ghana when we would meet them at the airport in
Accra. As we look back, Edgar and Mabel were not
nearly as old as we thought they were at the time.
However, we wonder if we would accept such a call
to Africa now that Normadeene and I are both in our
seventies.

Not long after our visit to Afrancho, we heard a
commotion outside of our house. Isaac and Benjamin
ran into the house shouting, "Chief Mensah and the
Queen Mother are here!" We stepped outside and
beheld a sight we will never forget. Chief Menasah
and the Queen Mother of Afrancho had traveled all
of the way from their village, along with his entire
entourage of elders, linguists, and court officials.

Yes, it was quite a sight to see! Chief Menasah
was being carried on a palanquin by several strong
men from his village. The Queen Mother also had
her own palanquin There were men and women
carrying gifts of bananas, pineapples, yams, and eggs.
They also brought us a rooster and a hen, which we
learned later were always part of such A ceremony.
Then, to top it all off, they brought us a big *Tom*
turkey which later became a close friend of our family
until the time we were forced to eat him. That is a
story all by itself.

We learned later that this was quite an honor.
Only special dignitaries were afforded this kind of
royal treatment. They had come to welcome us to
the Ashanti Territory and reciprocate my visit to their

village. The entire entourage crowded into the downstairs part of our house, the classroom part of our college. Our children stood wide-eyed as they observed pageantry they had never seen before and had not expected to see.

Protocol demanded that we greet them in the same way they had greeted me. I began by handing the Queen Mother a glass of water, *the drink for the weary traveler.* I offered the same to the rest of the entourage. She responded by pouring the glass of water on the floor. We had not expected that. I wish you could have seen the shocked look on the faces of our children. I then asked Chief Mensah, "What is your mission?" speaking through one of his linguists. He replied, "We have come to welcome you, and thank you for the mission you have come to accomplish." He went on to inform us of the dire need for Christian education in Ghana and offered his assistance to us in whatever needs we may have. He then motioned to several members of his entourage to present us with the gifts they had brought for us. We learned that these gifts were of great value to Chief Mensah and his people, as they did not have the worldly possessions we take for granted here in America. They demonstrated the fact that *you can give without loving, but you can not love without giving.*

We enthusiastically thanked Chief Mensah, the Queen Mother and their entourage for their expression of love for us. We promised to assist them in any way possible, and once again assured them we would try to get someone to establish a medical clinic in their village, as we had not yet received a response from the Nichols. When we received word that Edgar and Mabel had agreed to accept the call we had given them, we made a special trip to Afrancho to inform Chief Mensah. Once again He wept, but this time he wept for joy, as he knew many of his people, especially expectant mothers, would now receive the care they needed so badly.

I mentioned that the *turkey gift* was a story in itself. I was referring to the fact that it seemed like every morning, our new found pet, *Tom Turkey* was not satisfied with staying in our yard where he belonged. He would take off across the Accra Road to the little village of Susonsu. When we saw that he was across the road, we would yell for Benjamin and Isaac to bring the turkey back. They would respond, and our four children would join them in running in and out of the little huts in Susonsu yelling loudly at the turkey and trying to catch him. They were able to surround him and bring him back. This scene continued until the time we were to leave Kumasi and move to Accra. We were told by Isaac and Benjamin that we must eat *Tom Turkey* before we moved. They said that Chief Mensah would somehow know, and it would be an insult to him if we gave it to someone else. That was a sad time for our family, as we had all fallen in love with our friend, *Tom Turkey*. However, not wanting to offend Chief Mensah, we agreed to eat the turkey. The Duane Davenport family, from the Church of Christ Mission agreed to help cook him for the privilege of helping us eat him. Turkey was considered a delicacy in that part of the world.

We asked Isaac and Benjamin to take him far away from our house when they chopped *Turkey Tom's* head off. They agreed, but must have forgotten, as they did their dirty deed, to our horror, on the front steps of our house. I can still see that pet turkey running frantically around our compound without a head! The irony of it all was the fact that when we attempted to eat him, he seemed to become huge in our mouths, and proved to be so tough that it was impossible to chew *him*.

I mentioned earlier, that just outside of Kumasi, off of the road going east out of Kumasi, was a large mausoleum. It was guarded by two Ghanaian guards and two large, stone monumental lions. My curiosity was heightened each time we passed by on our way to Afrancho. It was covered with moss and vines, and had a rather foreboding air about it. I wondered what was inside that demanded protection by those guards. I was soon to find out what it was and how *curiosity some times kills the cat.* I was introduced to Korbina Kesi. He was well known in Kumasi as well as the rest of Ghana. He was a large man in his late fifties. He had the distinction of being the first Ambassador to Egypt from Ghana under the Kwami Nkruma regime. He took an immediate liking to me, and expressed that feeling by inviting Normadeene and the children and myself to his home for delicious meals on several occasions. He was a member of the proud Ashanti tribe. We found the Ghanaians to be rather closed mouths about many of their religious and social customs.

As we got better acquainted, we both felt free to ask questions, some of them very personal. I was eager to learn as much as possible from him about the Ashanti people and their religion and art. I sat spellbound as he painted beautiful word pictures of the history and tradition of his people. He told us about Osei Tutu and the golden stool that came down from heaven and helped found the Ashanti Akan culture. He told us of the importance of the most powerful of all of the Ghanaian kings, the Ashanti Hene, and later arranged an audience for us with the Ashanti Hene, Prempeh II. I have a beautiful picture, which I treasure, of Prempeh II and myself, which years after it was taken, helped me get back to Colorado from Duzeldorff, Germany, after celebrating the Twenty-fifth Anniversary of the founding of Ghana Christian College and Seminary. I will share that experience at a later time.

I asked him about the mausoleum outside of Kumasi. That opened the door for him to explain the custom of human sacrifice which, though not lawful, still continued while we were there. The authorities were instructed to *look the other way*. The Akan religion is very close to that of the old Egyptian pharaohs. They believe when a king or chief dies, they take their wives and entourage with them into the next world along with servants and other unfortunate ones who find themselves in the wrong place after the death of a king or chief. This may be where the phrase, *long live the king* had its origin, on the part of those who would be sacrificed. So long as the king lived, they were safe. However, when he died, they died with him and were buried with him.

When I first inquired about the mausoleum, he responded that there was more gold inside its walls than resided in our proverbial *Fort Knox*. He went on to say that because they had not been able to discover the method the Egyptians used for embalming their dead, they would encase the body of the deceased in solid gold. What he described must have been a magnificent sight to behold. I exclaimed to him, "I want to see that for myself!" I asked him if he could get me in. He replied, "I can get you in, but I can't get you out." It reminded me of the devil. He can get you into hell, but can't get you out.

Not long after Korbina Kesi told us about their custom of human sacrifice, there came a loud pounding on our door. It was about nine o'clock in the evening and we did not expect visitors that late at night. We opened the door and their stood an Englishman with a look of terror on his face. He begged us to let him in. He explained that he had just seen two men with a large knife and banana leaves chop off the head of a man alongside the Accra road. It so happened that the Oman Heni had died, and the *Adumfo*, under the spell of a special drug, were out finding men and women to fill the necessary quota of people to join him in the next world. There were thirty such deaths reported while we were there. We asked our *Christian* students how this could be? In a matter of fact way, they would respond, "That's our custom."

Many people have asked about human sacrifices, so I believe it would be fitting for me to share what Eva Meyerowitz records in her book *At the Court of an African King.* She had a first hand interview with an *Adumfohene,* Kofe Fifie by name. The following account of that interview is very enlightening, and I believe, in a way, explains the *matter of fact* attitude of our students when we confronted them with this issue. And also, even though wrong, just like the *suicide bomber's mind set* of 9/11, they were promised the same kind of rewards for their heinous deeds.

> One afternoon the Adumfohene Kofi Fofie, the chief of the executioners of human sacrifices, and his brother the Abrafohene Kodjo Adyaye, followed by two young assistants, came to see me in the rest-house to answer questions about their profession. They had permission from Nana to do so or they would not have talked, and it would have been impossible for me to get their ideas on the subject.

The Adumfohene, to my surprise, was a mild and kindly old man with nothing bloodthirsty or ferocious about him. On the contrary, his whole manner suggested the gentleman. I was therefore somewhat shocked, not that he had killed so many in his lifetime, but to hear that he liked his profession. He assured me that there was nothing horrifying about this, because people died for their own good. After all, life in heaven was much better than, or at least as good as, life on earth and, thanks to his great skill, the transit between life on earth and eternal life was very short indeed. Among the Akan, human sacrifice was largely connected with the life of the kings and queen mothers in the Other World. There life was thought to be much the same as on earth, except that there was no unpleasantness, no war no quarrels. The dead kings went to live in the city of the God Nyankopon on the sun, the dead queen mother joined their clan's goddess on the moon. There he reigned as on earth; it was their duty to continue to give 'life' to the people of their State. This they did on the one hand by helping the Sun-god and the Moon-goddess to shoot the life-giving rays of the sun and moon to earth, so that the crops should grow on which all life depends, and on the other, by acting as intermediaries between their people and the deities, so that they might receive support in times of need.

A king or queen mother can not reign without a court and personal servants; and for this reason many of the people who surrounded them on earth had to follow them into the Other World. Apart from slaves and prisoners of war, who were sacrificed to swell their retinue, most went of their own free will. In the case of the king, his most beloved son and daughter, many of his wives and his 'official friend', as well as some of his ministers and chiefs, voluntarily suffered sacrifice.

The palace personnel—cooks, stewards, cup-bearers and so on, each gave one member of their group so that the king might be well served in his new abode. In the case of the queenmother her husband had to follow her as well as her 'official friend' and those women elders who had loved her dearly. Slaves and prisoners of war, and above all, those criminals she had pardoned on account of their beauty, were also sacrificed to make her happy.

I noted all of these beliefs and customs with which I had been familiar as there was no secret about them. What I really wanted to know and did not dare to ask was, when did he last kill a human victim for sacrifice? Human sacrifice had been abolished by the British Government in 1901; but the custom still persisted secretly in many regions. The Kibi murder is a case in point. It greatly excited England in 1946. I came to know of another sacrifcial murder which also took place in 1946. At that time I was in Kumasi, and in bed with malaria, but in order to go on with my work I sent Kofi Antubam, who was then with me, to the house of an important Ashanti chief to make an

appointment for me in the following week,
meanwhile acquainting him with the
nature of my work.

When Kofi came to the house of the
chief he was told that the chief was dead
and had been buried the previous day. All
the ancient customs had been performed
in secret so that the Government did not
hear that human sacrifice had taken place.
The next day, Kofi was assured, a slave
descendant resembling the chief would take
his Government officials who were bound to
come to honor the dead. The substitute had
already been killed and his body prepared to
lie in state. Kofi was invited to see the corpse.
Apart from the voluntary victims who had
followed the Ashanti chief (probably none in
1946) there had also been others to ensure
his well-being in the beyond. These were
mostly people from the north who had come
to find work in Kumasi and were unaware that
the custom still existed to some extent in 1946.
They were waylaid at night on the roads and
murdered by the executioners. Their heads
cut off, put into bags and covered with cocoa
beans, and as 'cocoa' were transported on
lorries to Kumasi. At a later stage the heads
were buried with the chief. After a lull in the
conversation, the Adumfohene asked whether
I would like to see how it was done. I agreed
reluctantly, and the chief poured out a libation
and then dipped the point of his long
executioner's sword into the gin remaining
in his glass. He then pounced with great
suddenness on one of his young assistants

and, standing behind him, forced his head down. Then he lifted the sword. Luckily he did not forget himself but, at the last moment, reduced the force of the blow so that the sword landed gently on the young man's neck. He then showed me the exact spot where the sword had to cut through to sever the head from the body.

I realize that this is a rather graphic explanation of what we consider to be both inhuman and immoral. However, I believe it is good for us to realize how far superior the Christian religion is to what we just recounted and also to confirm how Christianity has served to do away with such practices.

This all took place some thirty-five years ago. We believe that this custom has long been abandoned due to the influence of Christianity as well as the law of the land.

By now, we realized that we would not be able to accomplish our mission of establishing an accredited Christian college in Kumasi, and also for the sake of our children's schooling. We were offered the Wyclif Translators house in Accra. We readily accepted the offer, as we needed to be near the Ministries offices there. Our Ashanti friends were not happy with this move as it would mean their young men and women would be far away from home in another territory. Accra is in the Gold Coast, with Accra the capital. Ga, rather than Twi is the native tongue there, even though English is the national language of Ghana. The difference is seen in the words for "thank you." It is Midawo ase Pi" in Twi, and "Oyiwaladon" in Ga.

Jerry with Chief Mensah
and elders in Afroncho

G.A. with baby named after him in Afroncho

Jerry with a friend from the
United Nations who was a World War II air
crewman, with the chief who was a World
War II Air crewman

Chapter IX

THE PISTOL

We had given Elder John Quansah's Takoradi address for our unaccompanied baggage. That included our car. We were anxious for it to arrive, especially our green Mercury Comet. We needed our own transportation badly, as it was too expensive to keep taking taxi cabs, and the government transport was far too time consuming. So we were elated when John Quansah sent word that the ship carrying our possessions had arrived in the Harbor at Takoradi.

Before we traveled to Takoradi, we also received word that the ship was not allowed to empty its cargo until the pistol and ammunition we had declared when going through Customs was removed from the ship and placed in safe keeping on shore. Normadeene had wrapped them up in blankets along with other bed clothes and put them in a large trunk. Our business manager, John Addo, agreed to travel to Takaradi, take a small boat out to the ship, locate the trunk in the hold of the ship, remove the pistol and give it to the Customs authorities for safe keeping.

It is interesting to note that we had been told not to trust the Ghanaians with our business dealings and especially with our money. That proved to be one of the biggest myths of all. We don't know what we would have done without John Addu. He was perfectly trustworthy and of great value to us.

He took care of all of the business dealing we had with Ghanaians. He helped us find a place to live, quarters for our college and students, and was of special help when new missionary families came to work with us. He would accompany us to the airport, and while we were greeting them, he would take care of their baggage and help them get through customs. He knew the language, and understood the monetary system. In short, he was a bit of an angel that watched over our family's interests.

He arrived back from Takoradi announcing that he had accomplished his mission. He found the pistol and ammunition, gave it to the authorities, and said they would notify us when our belongings were unloaded and ready to be retrieved.

About a week after John Addu returned from his mission to remove the pistol from the hold of the ship, we received word that we could claim our car and other unaccompanied baggage. We started for Takoradi early one morning via Government Transport. The roads were not paved and not maintained. Due to the large amount of rain, the bus wound its way through deep muddy ruts. The bridges left much to be desired. They were narrow, made of flimsy logs tied together by vine ropes. When the bridge spanned a deep gorge, we would hold our breath, as we could see in the valley below the wrecks of many vehicles that were not successful in their attempt to make it across. We passed through Dankwa, the village where Doug and Beth Keasling lived while serving as teachers for the Peace Corp. Little did we know how closely our lives and Christian service would intertwine in years to come, as Doug and Beth have been on the Board of Advisors of World-Wide Missions Outreach from its inception. Doug was the first Chairman of the Board.

The roads were not friendly to heavy vehicles. Our bus would sink all of the way to its axle in the glue-like mud. We had to get out every few yards and join in pushing that heavy *monster* of a vehicle out of those deep ruts. It was not long before we were covered with that mud from head to toe. There were mountain roads part of the way.

One of my problems was getting water that was safe to drink, and also food to keep up my strength. The fresh fruit which was readily available was my salvation, as I ate many bananas, mangos, and other delicious fruit on that journey to Takoradi.

The bus took us directly to the gate of the Customs buildings. When the dock workers saw us coming, they stopped work and stared at us. Any time a *bruni,* term for w*hite man,* came into the presence of a group of Africans, we stood out like a sore thumb. John Addo spoke to the foreman of the group and immediately he began to shout, "*Bra-ntemtem! Bra-ntemtem!*" "*Come quickly, Come quickly, the professor is going to speak to us!*" They wanted a sermon right there on the spot.

I told them of our mission and also that I had Bibles for them. After speaking for an hour or so, I got some Bibles out of my unaccompanied baggage and gave each of them one. It was like Christmas to them! They loved Bibles, and most of them could not afford to own one. We gave hundreds of Bibles to Ghanaian men and women who were hungry for the truth that Jesus Christ had for them.

We checked out our household goods and our green Comet. I would have to obtain a Ghanaian driver's license in the near future, obtain license plates, as well as auto insurance. But all of that would come later. It was time to redeem the pistol. It is important to call attention to the fact that all of this was very serious business for our Ghanaian hosts. They had serious looks on their faces and attempted to be as professional as possible. As we walked into the room where we would make our final declaration of goods, there, standing by a long desk, was a large Ghanaian man guarding the pistol. There was a tag attached to a wire identifying that firearm. As one considers the situation, we must realize that no guns are allowed in Ghana, except the ones used by the military. The police were not allowed to carry a firearm. A night stick was the extent of their armament. At that time we were unaware of this. As I moved closer to the gun, I had a startling revelation! I had a very difficult time keeping my composure. I wanted to laugh out loud! There on the desk, guarded closely by that big Ghanaian soldier, was a gun. But it was not *the gun.* It was our son G.A.'s toy pistol! If I had laughed I would probably still be in Ghana. It is important not to embarrass the government officials. I gazed at it in amazement, as my mind raced for an answer to my predicament. They announced that it would cost seventy-five Cedi, which was about one-hundred |American dollars at that time, to pay the duty on it. Also, I was informed I must have the necessary papers from *the powers to be* before I could take the pistol with me. I told them that I was not able to pay that much at that time. I asked them to secure it in a safe place until I could afford to redeem it. They agreed to that. They had sent the real pistol to the Wyclif Translators house where we would be living when we moved to Accra. As mentioned earlier, we found it necessary to be close to the various Ministries when we applied for accreditation for Ghana Christian College.

We loaded up the green Comet and started back

to Kumasi. Ghana was a British colony, so they drive on the opposite side of the road than we do in America. Getting back to Kumasi was an adventure in itself. We decided not to try to manage that muddy rutted road that the Government Transport bus wrestled. We took the long way along the Cape Coast road, through Accra and then north to Kumasi. Driving on the left side of the road proved to be a challenge, and quite a frightening one. When we came to Accra we went to the Wyclif house and were able to locate the trunk with the pistol. I took it out in the back yard and buried it deep. It is most likely still there to this day. The drive to Kumasi took us through the lush Rain Forest. I would travel that road many times.

Dean Howard Hayes of
Minnesota Bible College who urged
Jerry to bring a pistol to Ghana

Chapter X

ROLAND, THE ANGEL DOG

I made clear to the children that there was no way we could afford to have pets while we were in Ghana. That was going to be difficult. Our family always had at least one dog and several cats. Before leaving for Ghana, we purchased an *Iguana*, as we thought an exotic pet like that would help prepare the children for some of the creatures they would encounter there. He was a ferocious looking thing, like a small dinosaur. They named him *Iggy*. No matter how hard they begged, I insisted that we did not need any more mouths to feed.

One day a German doctor showed up at our door. He had with him a large *bush dog*. He explained that he had to return to Germany and could not take his dog back with him. His dog's name was Roland. I was not there at the time, but Normadeene, the good wife that she was, explained that her husband did not want us to have a dog, especially such a big dog with a large appetite. The doctor continued to tell her what a wonderful family dog Roland was, and that he especially loved children. He said he wanted to leave Roland with a family like ours that had children. He went on to say he hated to leave Roland in Ghana, but had no choice in the matter.

When I arrived home Normadeene related the story to me. I praised her for her firm stand and wise understanding of our situation. After all, we could not afford to feed such a large animal. We were having a difficult enough time feeding our perpetually hungry four children. Perpetually hungry is an under-statement. We were afraid the children would starve, as they were such finicky eaters. That changed the minute we left on the Pan Am jet for London. They were like locusts. They came in swarms and ate everything in sight.

Not long after, Pastor Drigger, a missionary for The Assembly of God Church, invited our family to his home in Kumasi for supper. The Driggers had several children and had the gift of hospitality. Pastor Drigger was a large man with a mild, soft spoken disposition. It is interesting to note that the denominational barriers that we often face in America, do not exist when you're far away from your home in a strange county. Being fellow Americans automatically bonded us together, and our doctrinal and theological differences did not seem to matter. We were all there for the same purpose of winning lost African souls to Christ. We were there for each other if the need arose. At least that was the *ideal.* However, later on, in Accra that principal did not hold true.

Our family, the six of us, settled down in the Drigger's large living room. I found a large stuffed chair in the corner of the room where I was almost out of sight. They had invited several other families to join us that evening. There were at least twenty people in all. This was a real treat for us, as the Driggers were able to obtain various foods that were unobtainable to us. They had been in Ghana long enough to know what was available and where to find it. Things that we take for granted in America, are often very difficult to find in Ghana.

As we sat there enjoying the Drigger's hospitality,

there came a knocking at the front door. It was the German doctor with his dog, Roland. As the doctor stood there, a strange thing happened. When he let go of Roland's leash, Roland eyed the people in the room, and then made a bee-line for me. He placed his head in my lap and looked up at me. I was hooked! The children did not have to plead, "Can we have him?" "He won't be any trouble. We will share our food with him. We will take care of him. You won't even know we have him." None of that was necessary as was the case with many of our past furry friends. Roland immediately became an integral part of the Gibson family. And may I add, a very valuable gift from God, as we learned in the months to follow. We came to consider him to be *our angel dog.*

BACK TO THE MAUSOLEUM

Try as I might, I could not get the mausoleum outside of Kumasi out of my mind. I went to bed at night fantasizing about the mysteries that were hidden behind its foreboding walls. I pondered about how I might be able to get in and out without being detected. I knew it would be risky business, but just being in Ghana was risky. It was a *once in a life time* opportunity, and I did not want to let it pass me by. I decided that before we moved to Accra I would at least make an attempt to see the splendors Korbina Kessi described to me.

It is strange now as I look back; it all seems like a dream. I decided to speak to Korbina Kessi and ask him for his wisdom on the matter. When I approached him, he was astonished at my request. His advice to me was to get the idea out of my mind! He said it is far too dangerous, and the odds were very slim, even if he could get me in, that I would ever see day light again. He plead with me to be satisfied with the word picture he had painted for me when I first asked him about it.

However, I persisted. I was determined not to tell Normadeene and the children about my obsession. I knew what they would say. I was finally able to get Korbina Kesi to join me in a plan to at least be able to see into the mausoleum without actually going inside. If I could get only one or two pictures from the entryway, that would be a feat no other white man had accomplished.

Korbina Kessi insisted that we must approach the mausoleum on a night when there was no moon. He would go to the front of the building and get the attention of the guards. While he was doing that, I would circle around through the thick underbrush that surrounded the mausoleum and hope the big iron gate was not locked.

The night came when we were to execute our carefully thought out plan. As I drove to pick up Korbina Kessi, a verse of Scripture entered my mind. I had been praying about this adventure for some time. Now God was speaking to me. The verse of Scripture that was ringing loud in my mind was I Corinthians 10: 9. "Do not tempt the Lord, as some of them did, and were destroyed by the serpents." That underbrush surrounding the mausoleum was infested with every kind of poison snake you could name. When I arrived at Korbina's house, I thanked him for his willingness to help, but related to him that Scripture in I Corinthians and told him I had decided to let what was inside the mausoleum remain a mystery. He breathed a loud sigh of relief. We prayed, and I returned to our house in Susonsu. I never did tell Normadeene and the children about what I *almost* attempted. In deed, *fools rush in where angels fear to tread.*

THE COMMUNION SERVICE

As I suggested earlier, we had a very good working relationship with the other missionaries in Ghana. I mentioned Duane Davenport, the Church of Christ missionary. We became very close friends, and even exchanged lectureships on several occasions.

One Lord's Day, Duane asked me to bring a sermon for his evening service. I agreed to do so, and looked forward to it with eager anticipation. We were to share communion with him and his congregation, also. That was wonderful, as he told me that if his supporting churches knew he was having that kind of fellowship with somebody outside of their *denominational* body, he would lose their support. I italicize the word d*enominational* because they claim to be non-denominational, but are far from that The Church of Christ *main liners* think it is a sin to use instrumental music in a worship service. I believe they are in error, but also believe they have a right to their beliefs, and certainly ought not violate their consciences. Roman 14:23 is clear on this. To our surprise, and I might add, to our delight, when we arrived at the church earlier than was expected, the Ghanaian congregation were singing and dancing to the accompaniment of loud drums and various other musical instruments. They somehow knew that we were not of the non-instrumental persuasion, so played and danced right on until a *lookout* warned them that the Davenports were coming. We got quite a chuckle out of that. There is no way you could ever get the sound of the drums out of their culture, and especially in their expression of worship.

It came time for *communion*. This was always very special, as we realized that this was one time when we were closely connected to Christians all over the world. It is a common *feast* that we all enjoyed, not separated by geographical borders. We could not find *grape juice* in Ghana, so we had to improvise. We used *Vim too,* a grape colored soft drink. Duane Davenport used fermented red wine. He had prepared the communion before the service. Somehow, nobody was keeping an eye on the communion. An old African man proceeded to drink up all of the communion. To him it was just good wine to drink. We have had many a chuckle over that incident, too.

Before leaving Kumasi, Duane Davenport hosted me to a round of golf. What I remember the most, is the fact that we had to send fore caddies down to the green, for vultures were waiting there to carry away our golf balls as they landed on the green. I also remember that if you missed the fairway, it was a lost ball. The rough was infested with poisonous snakes. Need I say more?

Becky and Roland with "Little Cat"
who she saved from being eaten

Becky and G.A. with our Angel Dog, Roland

Chapter XI

LIONS INTERNATIONAL AND

GOLF IN KUMASI

(Other friends we made)

I wish it were possible to paint an adequate word picture of *The Garden City,* Kumasi. The market place was a world of fantasy. Ghana is a *matriarchal* society. The lineage comes from the women's side of the family, not the man's. Therefore, when a king dies, his son does not become king, but his wife's brother's son. The British and others made the mistake of courting the favor of the wrong person until the found this out. As a result of this, the women own the property and control the purse strings. The market place is where the Ghanaian business women displayed and sold their wares.

As you walk through the market place it somehow reminds you of the bazaars at the carnival or county fairs. However, they are much more colorful and have much more to offer. The sounds and the smells have a profound effect on the atmosphere. It is like living in a dream. Most of the ladies have booths with tables on which their goods are displayed. As you walk by, they call to you in broken English, "Mister, I have a good bargain for you. Come and see!" If you see something you may desire to purchase, you point it out, and ask, "How much?" She will begin the *haggling* by asking a price far greater than the item is worth. You will step back and gasp, "Too dear! Too dear!" This means, too expensive. This *haggling* goes on until your reach a happy medium. The business ladies would feel insulted if you didn't go through the *haggling* ritual with them. For a price there is almost nothing that is not for sale in the market place.

Kumasi had a well kept zoo when we were there. Most of the lions, elephants and monkeys we saw while in Ghana were in that zoo. The flowers were magnificent! Fruit such as bananas, oranges, avocado pears and mangos grew wild. Exotic birds were everywhere, strutting their gorgeous colored plumage. In the midst of this beauty, by contrast, were the open gutters with raw sewage giving off an offensive stench that I can smell to this very day. In scriptural terms, "Behold, it stinketh!" The lack of adequate sanitation was one of the serious problems the health authorities of Ghana were forced to deal with. They neither had the adequate funds, technology or discipline back in 1966, when we were there, to deal with the problem. I mention this due to the fact that when one of us needed to find a *restroom* it always produced a crisis. I taught my family early on, that a person's intelligence is in direct proportion to his or her ability to adjust themselves to the situation at hand. We did plenty of adjusting while we were in Kumasi.

My friend, Duane Davenport did much to dispel the homesickness I may have experiences by taking me under his wings and sharing with me many of the things he had learned to do in the years he lived in Ghana before we arrived there. He took me to one of his Lion's lodge meetings and also took me as his guest to play golf on the only golf course in that part of Ghana, The Ashanti Country Club, as I named it. That was an experience I will long remember, due to the vultures on the greens I mentioned earlier.

OUR IRISH CONNECTION

One of the most memorable experiences we had while living in Kumasi was meeting some very special people from Ireland. Roy and Imer McDonald came to Ghana on a business trip and suffered drastically from *cultural shock* as they came directly to Kumasi by way of Accra without any kind or orientation. They had no idea of what they were in for. Fortunately for them, we met them at the market place and took them under our wing. They were Irish Catholic by birth, but as I have often said, God has no grandchildren. They were very interested in our mission, and eager to learn about what we believed and what message the students we trained in Ghana Christian College would preach.

Roy and Imer decided to be married while they were in Kumasi and asked me to perform the ceremony. They wanted to be married in a Catholic church, so contacted a group of Dutch Catholic priests who lived in a monastery on a hill over looking Kumasi. They agreed to allow them to be married in their chapel by a non denominational minister like myself. They also were very interested in the message we would teach our Bible college students.

Roy and Imer were a handsome couple. Roy was tall and strait with flaming red hair and flashing eyes that pierced right through you. Imer was of slight build but beautiful to behold. She had *raven black* hair and *emerald green* eyes. They both spoke with a thick Irish accent. We often wonder why they took to us as they did.

The road that took us up to the chapel wound up a hill that was covered with exotic flowers and strange multicolored birds. We were surprised to see the well kept, beautiful court yard in front of the chapel. The icons and tapestries that adorned the walls of the chapel were breath taking. We marveled over the fact that such a beautiful place existed in the midst of the poverty that surrounded it.

The ceremony was simple, but very beautiful. Normadeene served as the Maid of Honor, and a businessman friend of Roy's served as Best Man. I had the privilege of baptizing Roy and Imer a few days before their wedding. They were not denouncing their Irish Catholic heritage, they explained to the Dutch priests, but just confirming their faith and becoming better Catholics. The Dutch priests asked me to explain more about that to them.

The priests arranged a very lovely reception for Roy and Imer. That *put the icing on the cake,* for an experience and precious moment we will forever cherish. As we left to return home, they asked me to come back once a week to teach them what we teach our Bible college students. For six weeks before we moved to Accra I met with those men who were like sponges. They too, had a tremendous hunger for the truth. I often wonder what they did with the new Bible truths I taught them. They were particularly interested in what I taught them in regard to the conscience not being an informer, but an accuser. I told them the intellect informs, and the conscience accuses. Therefore, if our thinking is wrong, our conscience will also be wrong. I proceed to tell them that if men would investigate their faulty opinions, division in the church would cease, and Jesus' prayer for the unity of His people would be answered.

FOM-NYAMI, THE DOG THAT DID NOT FORGET

Shortly before we moved to Accra, the Adun's little black and white dog, Fom-nyami found the gate to the compound open and ran out into the path of an oncoming truck. The truck didn't even slow down. The poor little dog was writhing in pain. Normadeene and I ran out to see if we could help him. We had to be very careful, as any contact we made on his little body caused him much pain, and also we did not want to injure him further

Normadeene went back into the house and brought back a blanket. We carefully lifted him into the blanket and loaded him into the back seat of our car. Mrs. Adun and her children stood there watching. They did not know what to do and had a look a helpless look on their faces.

We asked Isaac and Benjamin where we could find a veterinarian? They said they would go with us, rather than give us directions. They expressed surprise over our concern for a dog. They said that most Ghanaians would just leave the dog in the road to die.

We drove around Kumasi and finally came to the compound of a veterinarian. He examined Fom-nyami and found that he had a broken leg, dislocated hip and badly bruised ribs. That explained why he was so sensitive to any touching of his little body. He relocated Fom-nyami's hip, set his broken leg and put a splint on it. He also wrapped his little body to protect his bruised ribs.

We returned home to a very grateful Adun family. They could not find the words to thank us enough.

We appreciated that, but the only thanks we really desired, was to see Fom-nyami whole again and free from pain.

I relate this story to you because of what happened several months later. After moving to Accra, we made several trips back to Kumasi, as I continued teaching Bible classes two days a week in the City Hotel. We had to pass by our old place of lodging owned by Mrs. Adun. We decided to stop by and greet the family. As we drove into the drive way, Fom-nyami came running out of the house wagging his tail and barking in a special thankful tone. He remembered us! He licked our hands and faces and expressed an excitement over seeing us that one seldom experiences in his or her life time.

That little dog never forgot the kindness we afforded him. There is no monetary payment that could come close to repaying our actions like the joy expressed by that little black and white dog when he saw us for the first time after his accident. Yes, the best things in life often times come in the most unexpected ways.

It is possible to give without loving but it is impossible to love without giving. Fom-nyami gave us the only gift he had. It was ample payment for any trouble we may have endured. However, in the words of Jeremiah Johnson, when he was asked about the inconvenience of taking care of a homeless boy, "It twern't any trouble." Coming to the aid of our *friend* Fom-nyami was one of the most satisfying experiences we had in Kumasi. One very significant thing I failed to mention, is the fact, that in the Ashanti Twi language, Fom-nyami means *gift from God.* I failed to mention a humorous incident that happened with Mrs. Adun when Chief Mensah brought us *Tom Turkey* from Afroncho. We think she may have been jealous, as she remarked, "We don't like turkey. We like chicken." We asked her why that was so? She replied, "Turkey has too much meat and not enough bones." We noticed that Isaac and Benjamin often chewed down the chicken bones. We surmised that was the reason for their beautiful white teeth.

Chapter XII

A STRATEGIC MOVE TO ACCRA

In spite of the protest of the chiefs and elders of the villages in the Ashanti Territory, we prayerfully, and with much deliberation, decided to make the headquarters of Ghana Christian College and Seminary in the Capitol city of the Gold Coast, Accra. Moses Addai was particularly upset with our decision because it would mean his son, Paul would have to find board and room at the college and would be far away from home. Moses was very outspoken and greatly feared due to his rough manner, and also due to his status in the line of Ashanti chiefs. He looked fierce and acted the part. Somehow, I gained his respect and he reluctantly agreed that it was imperative for us to locate in Accra. Accra was strategically located for what we needed to accomplish.

It was strategic for two basic reasons. First and foremost, it was near to the Ministries where the Minister of Education was stationed. If we were to be allowed to function as a licensed college in Ghana we would have to receive the authorization and necessary credentials from Kofi Vigbedor, the Minister of Education. I had traveled to Accra and met with him for over an hour. He was very cordial and also extremely interested in our mission. I described to him the kind of Christian college we desired to establish, and he agreed there was a great need for such a college in his country. The idea of training young men and women in the ministry who could reach their own people with the Gospel of Jesus Christ pleased him much. He pointed out how few Ghanaian young men and women would ever have the opportunity to attend a college in The United Kingdom or America. He vowed to help me in any way possible to make my dream come true.

I had heard that other Christian groups had been denied a license to do what I wanted to do. I asked Koft Vigbedor why he was eager to help me and not those who had come before me. He explained to me that his relationships with European missionaries had not been too pleasant. Any white person was classified as *European* to most Africans. He said, "Most of them seem to *tolerate* us. We can sense it." He went on to say, "You don't do that. You have a genuine love for me and the people of Ghana. You don't tolerate us. You love us." That was one of the finest complements I have ever received. If we are truly to walk like Jesus walked, we must never be *respecters of persons.* As much as possible, we must attempt to treat all people the same. We must not look at them through our own eyes. We must look at them through Jesus' eyes.(Romans 13:14)

As I look back more than thirty-five years, once again I understand the statement, *fools rush in where angels fear to tread.* For what Kofi Vigbedor demanded of me seems now to be an almost impossible task. Having received their independence from England in 1957, the government of Ghana was determined to prove to the world that Ghana was capable of excellence in every area of life, especially in the field of education. Every new institution of learning would be a showplace for the world to see. Nothing less than excellence would be acceptable to Kofi Vigbedor. I heartily agreed with him and assured him that the best was none too good for a Christian leadership training college.

What he asked of me was this. I was to begin by writing an essay explaining the mission and purpose of Ghana Christian College. I was to accompany that with a Constitution and Bylaws for the governing of the college which must conform to the basic standards laid down by the Ministry of Education.

He further instructed me to work out a four year curriculum to be taught and why each course was essential to our degree program. We were only allowed to present a Bachelors Degree program this time. I was told if this proved successful, we could petition to have a Masters and Doctoral program. I was also required to provide a staff of qualified teachers with a minimum of Masters Degree credentials. I had been corresponding with Cyril Simkins, who at that time was still in Northern Rhodesia with Moshoko Bible College. He had pioneered the work in Ghana with Max Ward Randell, and had a keen interest in what we were attempting to do. Also, Richard Hosstetter, who was also in Northern Rhodesia had contacted me about his desire to work with the college. With these men, we could teach a *core curriculum* of classes for at least the first two years. That way we could offer an Associates Arts Degree with that teaching staff. I would teach the Old Testament classes and the Hebrew language, Cyril Simkins would teach the New Testament classes and the Greek language, and Richard Hostetter would teach the general studies courses such as English, Psychology and other introductory courses. I included this information in my presentation to Kofi Vigbedor.

I was also instructed to provide a suitable *college campus* that would provide adequate housing as well as food for our students. It had to meet the excellent standards required of all new educational institutions. The government conducted regular inspections of all educational facilities in Ghana.

Kofi Vigbedor assured me, that if what I presented to him met with his approval, he would submit it to the entire staff of the Ministry of Education for their approval. He said that it would not be easy, but had a good chance of being approved. He wanted the material he required in his hands at least two weeks before we planned to conduct our first classes. I already had John Addu looking for a temporary campus to conduct our classes and feed and house our students.

The ten years I had taught at Minnesota Bible College proved to be invaluable to me in establishing a curriculum for the college. I had no problem with presenting the *mission and purpose* of the college, as the need for such a college to train African missionaries and evangelists burned deep in my heart. At the time I thought very little about my task. I could always feel God's strong hand on me as well as the guidance of His angels directing my every move.

It took me about two weeks of straining over my Smith Corona portable typewriter to produce the documents Kofi Vigbedor desired from me. He carefully scrutinized them, shared them with his colleagues, and not long after informed me of their approval. A week later he issued me a license to begin operating under the name Ghana Christian College. Oh, how sweet those words were to me!

The second reason for moving to Accra was so our children could attend Ghana International

School. It was the only school of its kind in the country, and it was of dire importance to us that our three oldest children could continue their high school education. Normadeene had agreed to *home school* Becky, but the three teenagers needed to be in a qualified educational institution. Gibby was a senior in high school. Cindy was a sophomore. And G.A. was in Seventh Grade.

Ghana International School was located in Accra near Flagstaff House on Airport Road. The only other alternative we had was to send them to Accra away from us and home, and have them receive their board and room at the school. That was out of the question, as it was difficult enough for the children to be so far away from our home in America, let alone be separated from us for at least nine months, only coming home for Christmas Break. One of the first things I would have to do after moving to Accra would be to enroll Gibby, Cindy and G.A. in Ghana International School.

The day finally came when we loaded up our little green Mercury Comet and headed south on Accra road to our new home in Tesano in the Wycliff Translator's headquarters, where we would live until we returned to America. The Accra Road left much to be desired. It circled south east through the Rain Forest. We went through many small villages where chickens, pigs, sheep, goats and people walked down the middle of the narrow streets with open foul smelling gutters, always having the right of way. The *mountain stream* like road was not the biggest problem. Our *angel dog* Roland along with Gibby, Cindy and G.A. piled into the back seat of the little green Comet. The comet did not have air conditioning, and that was bad in itself, as the heat driving through the Rain Forest was stifling. However, Roland added to that discomfort with a *popcorn-like* odor that permeated the entire car. There were several large towns, such as Nkawkaw and Koforidua, between Kumasi and Accra. We would travel through these towns often in the future, as we returned to teach classes in Kumasi. Koforidua became indelibly stamped in our minds. It was at about the half-way point of our journey. By the time we arrived there, the children had already been complaining, "We're hungry, when can we stop and eat?", for many miles. On the sides of the narrow streets were many food vendors. We had no idea what their food was like, or how safe it may be for Americans like us to eat. We usually confined our eating to fresh fruits and vegetables. However, there comes a time when you are so hungry, that your standards of what is sanitary and what is not sanitary drops to a very low level. We noticed one vendor selling large doughnut hole like pastries. We inquired as to what they were. He told us they were b*oefruit* and went on to say they were very delicious. They smelled good and looked good, so for several *pesewa* we purchased enough so we could each have two. We also purchased some soft drinks referred to as *mineral* by the natives.

The *boefruit* went down easy as we washed it down with our *minerals*. However, by the time we got to Aburi, John Addu's home town, the Capitol City of the proud Aquapim tribe, we all became deathly sick. We learned later that this was the place where Kwami Nkruma had his Winter Retreat. John Addu never let the opportunity go by to tell us he was an Aquapim. None of that was of any consequence to us now. We were in deep trouble. We needed rest stops right now! We needed them every five minutes, but they were nowhere to be found. We lost all of our dignity, and suddenly practiced the wise suggestion,

"When in Rome, do like the Romans," but changed it to "When in Ghana!" I would stop the car and we would run into the bushes. Fortunately we had enough sense to carry toilet paper with us when we traveled. As was the case when the children came down with Malaria, first they thought they were going to die, and then they were afraid they would not die. We were going out of both ends. We later discovered that the vendor who sold us the *boefruit* had deep fried it in *spoiled palm oil.*

We arrived at the Wycliff translators house in Tesano late that afternoon. We were all too sick to even think about unloading the car. Roland was the only one in our *family* well enough to enjoy our new home. I might add, he immediately made himself at home. We were about to begin a new adventure. Our angel was still with us. We were too soon to encounter him. I said *him,* even though the term *angel* is neuter gender, because the angel that appeared to Normadeene and me had the form and face of a man.

Chapter XIII

GETTING ESTABLISHED IN ACCRA

(Ghana International School)

The first order of business, after getting settled in our new place of abode, was to get our children enrolled in Ghana International School. We loaded them into the little green Comet and drove through some very interesting country side to the place where the school was located, not far from Flagstaff House, the headquarters of Ghana's military forces. We drove by Achimota, where many of Ghana's government officials and educators received their formal education. The beloved Dr. Joseph Danquah taught there.

We were impressed at what we found. Ghana International School was housed on a finely groomed campus with attractive, well kept class room buildings, as well as an administration building and cafeteria. We climbed up the steps leading to the reception desk in the administration building. We were met by a very friendly receptionist with a strong British accent, who greeted us cordially. I informed her of our desire to enroll our three oldest children in their school. The receptionist left the room and came back with a raft of forms and asked us to complete them. Also, we were informed of the tuition fees that would be required if our children were found qualified and allowed to enroll.

Upon completing the enrollment forms, Gibby, Cindy and G.A. were led away into a room where they were to be given Ghana International School's entrance exams. They were in for the surprise of their young lives. We did not realize that, due to the fact the school was administrated by British educators, the school followed the British *form system* of education. What that meant is that the students started with a particular subject in an earlier *form* and then continue that subject from a higher *form* to a higher *form* for the rest of their time in school. That way they would increase their proficiency in math, history, a foreign language, or any other subject, by the time they reached their final *form* which would be equal to being a Senior in one of our high schools. The children did the best they could under the circumstances. They complained that they had never studied most of the subjects for which they were tested

We were then ushered into the office of the Head Mistress, Mrs. Inman. She was a very gracious lady, in her mid fifties, who gave off an air of British dignity. She too spoke with a strong British accent. She proceeded to inform us as to the basic rules of conduct expected from the students enrolled in her institution. She further informed us that there was no guarantee that our children would be admitted. That would depend upon how they fared with their entrance exams. She said we would be informed by mail what her decision would be, as she had the final say so. We drove back to Tesano with high hopes. It was imperative that our three oldest children be allowed to further their education while we were in Ghana. There was no way Normadeene could *home school* all four of them. They needed to be kept busy in order to allow Normadeene and me to be about

our business of establishing Ghana Christian
College. It is a true saying that "An idol mind is the
devil's workshop". There is no telling what those
three might have conjured up had they been left
alone with that much time on their hands.

Several weeks went by, and then one morning
when I picked up our mail at the post office in down
town Accra, I found a letter from Ghana International
School written by Head Mistress, Mrs. Inman. She
regretted to inform me that she would be unable to
admit our children for enrollment in her school as
they had failed their entrance exams. She went on to
say that if I had any further questions she would be
happy to grant me an audience. This was devastating
news! How could I tell the children? What would
this do to their self esteem? What would they do all
day long for months on end? There was no way I
could take Mrs. Inman's letter as final!

I jumped into the little green Comet and headed
for Ghana International School. I am embarrassed
to admit that I was a little hot under the collar when
I approached the desk of the receptionist demanding
a meeting with Mrs. Inman. She insisted I must make
an appointment before I could see her as her
schedule was full for that day. I insisted that that
was not satisfactory and demanded an audience right
now! Mrs. Inman must have heard the exchange with
her receptionist, as she opened the door to her office
and inquired if she could be of any assistance. Then
she recognized me, and I am sure she knew why I
was there.

She politely, but rather nervously, invited me into
her office. She proceeded to explain that she had no
recourse due to the results of their failed entrance
exams. When she was done speaking I asked her.
"Mrs. Inman, if I were to give you an exam in the

Hebrew

Hebrew or Greek language could you pass it?" She replied, "Of course not!" I asked her then, "How did you expect our children to pass an exam on subjects they had never studied?" She agreed that I had a point. I asked her if she would be willing to admit our children on a probationary status. If they were not able to catch up to the rest of the students in their classes, then she could dismiss them. But I went on to ask her to at least give them a chance. A loud silence followed. I could see that she was very much troubled by the situation she was facing. After a minute or so, she looked into my eyes and said, "Alright, I think it is only fair that we give them an opportunity to prove themselves. But I hope you will not be too disappointed if they are not able to achieve the standards we require of them." I gave a sigh of relief and thanked her for changing her mind.

We never told the children that they had been rejected. That would have crushed their self esteem. Being so far away from home was bad enough in itself. But being rejected from Ghana International School would have been more than they could handle.

To make a long story short, the children fit right into the program of the school. They were fast learners, and in no time at all were on the same level as all of the rest of students in their classes. It is especially gratifying to tell you that when the time came that we had to return to America we received a beautiful letter from Mrs. Inman expressing what a great contribution our children had made to the over all program of the school, and telling us how much they would be missed. Incidentally, G.A. had French as one of his subjects, which he had not studied before enrolling in Ghana International School. He won the *form prize* in French for that school year.

I compared the letter we had received from Mrs. Inman refusing our children admittance into her school with the letter she sent referred to above. What a difference a few months makes some time!

Normadeene in a native African dress

Chapter XIV

OUR HOME IN ACCRA

Wycliff Translators House

The Wycliff Translators House, in which we were to live until we returned to the States, was a beautiful, white, two story structure. The street in front of the house was not paved, but the surface was smooth, which kept it from being dusty like a gravel road would be. As you drove down the street to our house, you passed by several well kept bungalows, as they were referred to by the *Europeans* who lived in them. Each house was guarded by a tall stone wall, which in turn was guarded by hundreds of pieces of broken glass and other sharp objects, intended to slow down any would be intruders. Each house also had a strong gate that led one into a beautiful court yard. At the time, I mused over the fact that nothing like that was ever necessary in our safe and secure neighborhoods in America. That was long before 9/11 though, after which one will never feel so safe and secure.

The court yard which surrounded our house was magnificent! Upon entering the compound, you were greeted by a beautiful rock garden with a pool and water falls. There were beautiful, exotic tropical fish swimming in the pool. Flower laden vines climbed lazily up the walls of the stairs, just behind the rock garden, that led to the upstairs apartment. I was rather embarrassed at first, as I thought of the people back home who were supporting our mission, who thought we were living in primitive conditions, when the fact was that we were living in much nicer accommodations than we enjoyed back in the states. However, there were several drawbacks that I will point out at a later time. We had the downstairs apartment, that had a small porch as well as a car port just to the right of the porch. We were fascinated by the many different colored and different sized lizards that ran back and forth on the top of the compound walls. Also, there were trees pregnant with every kind of tropical fruit imaginable, from mangos, avocado pears and oranges to bananas.

I failed to mention that most of the compounds occupied by Europeans on our street were guarded day and night by a hired security guard. Roland, our *angel dog,* served us well as our security guard. While we were there every house on the block had been robbed several times, in spite of the dangerous sharp objects on top of their walls and the security guards that were there to protect them. We never lost a thing as God was true to His promise and sent His angels to watch over us by day and by night. Psalms 34:7 and 91:11.

As secure as the large iron gates were by themselves, with the added security of a human guard, several times those desiring to enter their compound were met by another, more deadly security guard. As one of the guards attempted to open the gates to the compound he was guarding, he was confronted by a giant *Green Momba,* one of the most deadly snakes in all of Africa, that had wrapped himself securely around the metal spokes of the gate. We heard of several guards who had lost their lives while attempting to open a gate guarded by a poisonous viper whose venom kills in a matter of minutes.

The layout of the interior of the Wycliff translators house was rather unique. As you entered, immediately to your left was a living room and an archway that led to the dining room. The floors were made of beautiful colored pieces of marble like terracotta. A long hall way stretched down to the right of the living room, and four bed rooms were positioned along the right side of the hall way. At the end of the hall way on the right side of the building was a room with a commode, and the last room on the right had a bath tub and shower. I mentioned some drawbacks to our house earlier, one of which was the fact that there were many times when there was no water for bathing or flushing the commode. To the left at the end of the hall way was a door that led to the kitchen. It was separated from the dining room by a wall with a small service window where dishes and food could be passed through. We had many memorable occasions as well as very interesting meals in that dining room. Due to some very important experiences we had while living there, knowing the lay out of the house will be helpful.

The first bedroom to the right coming in from the front door was Gibby's room. It was furnished by our land lords with a twin bed, dresser and chair. We were able to find a small fan for each of the children's bed rooms to circulate the air. The next room down the hall was G.A.'s room. It had the same furnishings as Gibby's room. The next room was the Master bed room, Normadeene's and my room. We had a queen size bed with a firm mattress, along with a 4000 B.T.U. air conditioner shipped to us by Montgomery Wards in St. Paul, Minnesota. The bed came first and then later the air conditioner arrived. We knew that due to the rigorous schedule, it was imperative that we get a good night of rest. Once again, we had pangs of guilt, as we would like to have been able to afford air conditioners in each of the children's rooms. However, the small fans served them well, and they adjusted to the climate and seemed to have no problem sleeping.

The last bedroom down the hall, after our bedroom, was shared by Cindy and Becky. It was furnished with twin beds, and a small dresser and chair for each of them, along with the small fan I mentioned earlier. The location of the rooms is important, as I suggested earlier, due to a very traumatic experience we had later on.

We mentioned the many colored lizards that paraded up and down the compound walls like miniature dinosaurs. They seemed to have a dance routine, as they would, run, stop, and then bob their heads up and down, and start over again.

We did not mind them on the outside wall so much, but we did not like to have them in the house. However, they liked being in the house and were able to find a way to get in. Benjamin and Isaac assured us they would do us no harm, but on the contrary were welcome guests, as they ate spiders and other insects such as the malaria mosquito that we had to constantly be on guard for. We were to take a pill every morning at the breakfast table to prevent our contacting the disease. Every now and then I would find an unused pill, left there by one to the children. Sure, enough, they would soon after come down with an attack of malaria. Everyone in our family came down with malaria while we were in Ghana, except me. My angel even guided the mosquitoes away from me.

Even though I relented in regard to having a dog, due to Roland's special meeting with me, I insisted, we could not afford to have any other pets, especially a cat. A little girl that Becky became close friends with, who we called *the peanut girl*, because she carried a large basket of little clusters of peanuts on her head, that she sold for a pesewa, brought a little black and white cat, with a bulls eye circle around its right eye and gave it to Becky. Becky brought it into the house and with here sweetest begging tone asked if she could keep it. I responded, "No way!" with as firm a tone of voice I could muster. She went back out and came back in crying profusely. She said, "If we don't take it, they are going to eat it!" Needless to say, we now had a both a dog and a cat.

We had to go down town in Accra and rent a mail box at the post office, as well as orient ourselves to the stores and other facilities available to us. Going down town to the post office became a daily routine for us, and turned out to be one of the major sources of enjoyment while we were in Ghana. Just getting there was a major undertaking. We were still not used to driving on the left hand side of the road, and the lack of stop lights, with traffic circles to take their place was also difficult for us to get used to. Each traffic circle had its own special significance. The first one we encountered on our way to the post office was called February 24th Circle, commemorating the coup that overcame the Nkrumah regime, that made possible our coming to Ghana. The second one was March 5, 1957 Circle commemorating what to them was equal to our Fourth of July, for that is when Ghana received her independence from England.

There was much traffic congestion, so we eeked our way down to the final traffic circle that had no name, but put us in the heart of what we would call *downtown Accra.*

One of the first things I noticed, off to the left, as we entered the traffic circle was a large Anglican church. That church later served us well in a situation we got ourselves into. One of the things you may have wondered about is where did we get gasoline for our automobile? As I recall, there were two gas stations on our way to the post office. The first one was located in The Government Transport parking lot, that also housed many other private transportation firms. It was a Shell *petro* station. We found that the British gallon was from the *metric* system and was larger than our U.S. gallon. Gasoline prices in Ghana were comparable to what we have to pay today in America. Then, further on, there was a British Petroleum station. None of them were full service, and none of them offered oil and lube service. We could purchase gas and oil, but that was all. I failed to mention, that on the way down to the post offices, we always passed the large Kingsway store, which was similar to our department stores. You could purchase almost anything there, both dry goods and perishables.

Outside of picking up our mail at the post office, the most significant event that took place when we were there, was our meeting with Mr. Matani and his son Lal. The cirlce, which reminded us of the Square found in many of our towns, was lined with small shops of every kind and size and shape. They were colorful and fascinating to walk by. But even more fascinating to enter and observe first hand the merchandise being trafficked there. One such store was operated by Mr.Matani and his son Lal. It seemed to be *love at first sight* as Mr. Matani immediately took a strong liking for our family. Even though Becky was seven years old, he referred to her as *Baby*. It was always hot and humid in Accra, so when we entered Mr. Matani's store, which featured shirts and sox and trousers, he always offered us some *mineral* which we mentioned earlier was equivalent to our soda pop. He had coca cola, but the children's favorite was *Vim to*, a drink made out of various fruit juices. I mentioned Mr. Matani, as he played a very important part in our mission.

Mr. Matani often invited us into his home where he called in the chefs from the Taj Mahal restaurant to prepare us delicious Indian food. He and Lal were from India and were Hindus by birth. However, they were very open to our teaching them about Jesus.

Another thing we did, immediately upon moving to Accra, was to get acquainted and establish friendships with various government officials and law enforcement officers. We introduced ourselves to Mr. Asmah, the Chief Customs Officer of Ghana, and at his request, met with him each week for a prayer meeting in his office. He became a very valuable and beloved friend of our family as well as Ghana Christian College.

We also met Chief Agbete, Chief of Police for the Nima Police Station near the site of our college. He too proved to be a valuable and trusted friend. His right hand man, Kojo, a powerful, giant of a man, also became our close friend. We invited them to our home for refreshments whenever they were in our area, an invitation of which, to our delight, they often took advantage. We have some beautiful pictures of some of the times they were with us.

We noticed that Chief Agbete was attired in a khaki uniform and Kojo in a black uniform, which seemed to be very hot. We found out that the *literate* policeman wore khaki and the illiterate policemen wore black. Even though English was the national language of Ghana, due to its long British rule, only thirty percent of the people of Ghana could speak English.

The day came when our air conditioner finally arrived from the States. I mustered up several strong bodied students to help install it in the window of our bed room. It was large and heavy and awkward to handle. The electricity in Ghana was 220 volts, which was good for the air conditioner, for it was wired f or that. However, for many of our other household appliances, we had to have *step down* transformers to accommodate for the difference in voltage.

The students and I were able to make room for the cumbersome air conditioner in the window, but just barely. It would be a tight fit. Somehow, the unit was too heavy for all of us to pick up and place in the window space. As we were grunting and straining, Kojo pulled up in his police car. He had come for refreshments. I yelled for him to come on in. As he entered the room, he asked, "What is the problem?" We told him we wanted to place the air conditioner in the window space. He looked at it and asked, "Do you mean like this." He reached down, picked up the heavy air conditioner, and to all of our amazement, gently placed it in the window space. At that moment, he was one of our angels who came just in the nick of time.

I commissioned several of our students to find a suitable place that we could rent for conducting the business of Ghana Christian College. We needed a place that not only had class room space, but also had a kitchen and could house students. I promised the students I had been teaching in Kumasi that I would drive up to Kumasi every other week and conduct special classes on both the Old and New Testaments. This was because several of them were unable to join the college in Accra. I planned on doing this until we were able to start classes at our new location. I was hoping they would find a suitable place while I was gone.

Jerry & Becky by the Wycliff Transator's
House in Accra

Chapter XV

BACK TO KUMASI

Early one morning, John Addu and I headed back for Kumasi in the little green Comet. This was the first time we had traveled that way since picking up the car in Takoradi. We drove out of town on what was called the Tema Freeway and headed east toward Aburi, John's home town.

As we drove along John shouted, "Stop the car!" I stopped and he jumped out and started chasing a giant lizard which he saw crossing the road ahead of us. It was big and clumsy and looked like a crocodile. It headed for the ditch and disappeared into a large culvert. John lost it and was very disappointed. He explained to me that it was a giant *Mampam.* He said they were much desired and would bring a large amount of money in the market place. I later had the experience of eating *Mampam* and John was right. It was delicious. I have often wondered how John would have been able to wrestle and subdue that ferocious reptile. I never asked him, though.

The further northeast we traveled the more mountainous the terrain became. Aburi was situated in the mountains and for that reason was an escape haven from the heat of the Accra plain which we were leaving. Instead of being one-hundred degrees, it was only ninety degrees in Aburi. I understood why Kwami Nkruma used this village for a summer retreat.

Aburi was one of the few places where we saw monkeys in the trees as well as many exotic, beautifully colored birds. Parrots were to be seen everywhere, and I remarked to John that our family would like to own a parrot. He advised me that the *West African Gray* parrots that we were seeing were the most sought after of all parrots, as they were the best talkers and made wonderful pets. He promised to bring one of them to us some day. I wondered if he would do so.

As we drove on, the road became very narrow and difficult to manage. The bridges that crossed deep ravines were usually a few logs placed side by side and end to end with not much holding them up. We passed by many giant ant hills that John told me housed millions of *army ants*. He said their sting was worse than that of a bee, but the adobe that made up the ant hill was excellent for making building blocks for brick houses.

Even though the actual miles we traveled were about two-hundred and seventy-six, It took most of the day for us to reach Kumasi. We arrived at the City Hotel, where I had made reservations, late in the afternoon. I had reserved a room in the hotel for our classes also. We were scheduled to have our first class from 7:00 P:M. to 9:P:M. that evening. We would resume classes at 8:00AM the next morning and continue until 4:PM in the afternoon.

I checked in at the front desk and was greeted by a very well dressed young Ghanaian man. He had a bright smile on his face and assured me they would do everything in their power to make my stay in their hotel a memorable one. I doubt very much that he really knew what he was saying at the time, because what was to follow made it an experience I will not forget as long as I live.

A bell hop led the way to the elevator. My room was on the second floor. He took my bags to the door of my room, gave me the key, and after I gave him a couple cedis tip, he cheerfully returned to the elevator. I opened the door to my room and walked in. There, sitting on the side of my bed, was a very beautiful, scantily clad young Ghanaian woman, perhaps in her early twenties. I must have had a shocked look on my face as she rose from the bed and came toward me to embrace me. I was not prepared for this. I could smell palm wine on her breath and her eyes had a blurry look in them. I realized now what the desk manager meant when he said they wanted my stay to be a memorable occasion. I wasn't going to forget this very soon. I was the *county boy* of all *country boys* at this stage in my life. I still am when things like what was happening there is concerned. I was a married man with four children. And on top of all of that I was a preacher of the Gospel. But most important of all, I was a Christian. I wonder if that young Ghanaian woman had any idea as to who it was she was attempting to seduce, or what predicament she might be finding for herself. I was there in Kumasi primarily to prevent such scenes like this to happen in the lives of God's children.

I stretched my arms out arms length and pushed her away, and at the same time the words, "I'm in a big hurry. I have to meet some friends in a few minutes for dinner!" came blurting out of my mouth. I wanted to preach at her, but I doubt that she could have understand a word I would say. This is one time when actions spoke much louder than words. I ushered her to the door and closed it after her. I then went into the bathroom to freshen up. On the way down to the dining room, I stopped by the front desk and rehearsed what had happened with the young woman in my room. The desk clerk apologized and apologized. He went on to tell me that most of the *European business men who stay at their hotel desire such companionship.* He said the girl in my room was from a very poor family and was attempting to make money for furthering her education. He assured me that it would never happen again.

My classes went well. We left for Accra early the next morning, and were back in Tesano in the early afternoon. Our trip was uneventful, except for two young Ghanaian girls who were standing by the side of the road, outside of a little village, stark naked, accept for being covered from head to toes with a white chalk like paint. They were gyrating their bodies back and forth. I asked John, "What are they doing?" He smiled and answered, "They're dancing." I later learned that they most likely had just been initiated into their tribe and what they were doing was part of their *puberty rights.*

All of the way back I tried to think of how I would tell Normadeene about the beautiful young Ghanaian woman in my hotel room. Maybe I would not tell her at all. Normadeene is not a jealous woman, and I have made it a point to never give her a reason to be jealous. However, after answering her questions about our travel to and from Kumasi and how the classes went, I shared with her my *Potipher's Wife* experience. Both of us wondered if there was some way we could help that young lady further her education without selling her body.

Normadeene and Becky
at The City Hotel in Kumasi

African girls on Accra Road at time of their
"Rite of Passage"

Normadeene with Mabel Nichols in Kumasi

Chapter XVI

GETTING STARTED IN ACCRA

There were several urgent things that faced us in order to start classes in the Fall semester. And there were other things we wanted to accomplish that may not have been quite so urgent. The first order of business was to call qualified, dedicated professors to man our class rooms. I had contacted Cyril Simkins, who at that time was a professor at Mashoko Bible College in what was then known as Northern Rhodesia. He told me of another man, Richard Hostetter who had expressed a keen interest in becoming a part of the Ghana Christian College teaching staff. We had a minimum requirement for our teachers of at least a Masters Degree in their area of teaching. Both of these men met that requirement. After much prayer and deliberation, Cyril Simkins came to Ghana with his wife Mary and daughter Mary Anne.

Some time later Richard Hostetter agreed to join the college staff and came to Ghana with his wife Nancy, two young sons, Steve and Jeff and baby daughter, Heather. We were delighted to be able to inform Minister of Education, Kofi Vigbedor that we had a qualified staff that was able to cover the curriculum necessary for our first year of classes. Both of these families arrived in Ghana in time for classes to begin. Cyril would teach the New

Testament classes and Greek. Richard would
General Survey courses and English and I would
teach Orientation, the Old Testament and Hebrew.
This proved to work very well.

Our next order of business was to find a suitable
place to administrate the business of the college,
house and feed students and conduct our classes.
While I was away in Kumasi, Isaac and Benjamin
found a prospective place that I would look into. It
was owned by a Ghanaian business woman. Ghana
is a *matriarchal* society. That means that the lineage
of a family comes from the mother's side of the family,
rather that the man's. When a chief died, his oldest
son did not succeed him. His wife's brother's son
became the next chief. I referred to this custom
earlier.

The more I learned about the Akan culture, and
that of Ghana as a whole, the more I developed a
keen desire to learn and understand it. I decided, if
possible, I would enroll in The University of Ghana
in Legon and seek a degree in African Studies. I
wanted to learn about Africa and her people from
the African viewpoint and mind set, rather than the
traditional European viewpoint that was taught in
most colleges and universities.

Then, of course, you can't have a college without
students. We required the equivalent of a high school
diploma and the passing of a standard entrance exam
for a student to be admitted into the college. I was
constantly working at finding qualified men and
women, both old and young, to recruit. I met one of
my first recruits while negotiating for a place for our
college to meet.

Cindy, Gibby and G.A. in front of
Ghana International School

Cindy, G.A. and Gibby nearing Graduation Day
at Ghana International School

Chapter XVII

FINDING A PLACE TO HOUSE

OUR COLLEGE

We found a place near Nima, that we believed would serve us well until we were able to have a campus of our own. I drove to the office of the Ghanaian business woman with whom I was to negotiate a lease. When I arrived there, I found myself waiting inside the compound that surrounded her office building. I believe she deliberately left me waiting as a means to show me that she was in charge and had the authority to either accept or reject us as a tenant. As I have suggested earlier, Ghana is a society where the woman own the property, have the money and conduct the business, just like in America. Of course I am joking.

While I was waiting for an audience with the land lord, a young man approached me in a tricycle like vehicle propelled by his arms. I noticed that his upper body looked strong and muscular. However, his legs and feet dangled down, completely useless. I introduced myself to him as Professor Jerry Gibson from Ghana Christian College. He replied by introducing himself as Christian Adjei. He then went on to explain to me the reason for his handicap. He said that a missionary doctor gave him shots in the hips when he was a young child, and it rendered his legs paralyzed and useless for life. He continued

141

to explain how he had completed a course from The University of London to be a secretary or stenographer, but could not find a job due to his handicap. I believe he was having a fine *pity* party. He spoke with a booming voice. Without thinking, I asked him, "Have you ever thought about being a preacher?" He laughed and said he had never given it a thought. I told him I just happened to have a Prospectus for Ghana Christian College in my car, and would like to leave it with him. I retrieved it from the car and came back and placed it in his lap. He took it with a smile, but didn't sound too interested in becoming a preacher of the Gospel. I did not ask him his religious background. I learned, long ago, to start with people where I find them, not where I want them to be. It was a matter of first things first. We could deal with his relationship to God at a later time.

I completed my business with the land lord, and signed a one year lease for the building we desired for our college. I recall that the rent was rather high for my budget, but Cyril Simkins and Richard Hostetter agreed to share the expense with me. I had one more class at the City Hotel in Kumasi, so the next morning feeling very satisfied with the place we had for classes in Accra, I left with John Addu for Kumasi.

The journey to Kumasi was uneventful. My last class went very well. I was not met by a Ghanaian woman in my room, and was greeted by more apologies from the front desk However, something happened that made a lasting impression on my mind.

As I prepared to start my afternoon class, I was approached by a young Ghanaian man named Elijah. He asked me if he could wash my car while I was busy teaching my class. I saw no reasons for not accepting his offer, as it had been a long time since the little green Comet had the dirt, mud and grime washed off of her.

While I was in the middle of my lecture there came a nock on the door. It was Elijah. He wanted the keys to the Comet so he could dust and sweep out the inside. Without hesitating, I reached into my pocket, handed him the keys, and went right on teaching my class.

After the usual farewells and exchange of gifts, I went out to get into my car. I was anxious to see how it looked after just having a long, much needed bath. To my dismay, it was not there. Neither was Elijah to be found! I was in a dilemma. What was I to do? I was staying one more night in The City Hotel and planned to drive back to Accra the next morning.

John Addu proceeded to admonish that I should never have trusted an Ashanti with the keys to my car. "That would never happen in Aburi!," he proudly proclaimed. I told him, and the crowd of students and by standers that had gathered, to be patient. There must be a logical explanation to my problem. They all agreed, and the logical explanation they agreed on was that Elijah was a thief and had plain and simply stolen my car! I was about to learn a sad lesson. I found that there was very little tolerance among the native Ghanaians, one for another. I learned very early that if you heard somebody call, "Thief!" you should not move, but stop in your tracks. For if you started running for any reason whatever, the mob would pile on you, assuming you were the culprit, and almost beat you to death before the law enforcement authorities arrived on the scene.

I waited for at least a half an hour, which at the time seemed like an eternity, for Elijah to come back with my car. John Addu kept insisting we take a cab to the police station and report that my car had been stolen. Finally, I decided that was my only course of action. We arrived at the police station and were met by a giant, *Pun Jab* looking police officer. He was dressed in black, so was illiterate. I rehearsed to him my problem. He took me into the Chief of Police, who had me tell what happened, once again. He immediately assured me that he would have my car back for me in a very short time. He went on to apologize for my inconvenience and assured me the young man would be apprehended and punished severely for his crime. I did not realize, just how severely, he was talking about at the time.

The Chief of Police and his officer took us back to the Hotel, and as we drove up Elijah came around the traffic circle with my car. Without asking any questions, the big, burley police officer dragged Elijah out of the car with such force that it sent him realing onto the ground. He then took out a big, black night stick and began to beat Elijah unmercifully! Elijah would attempt to get up on his knees, but the policeman kept beating him down. The officer stopped and asked me, "Shall I beat him some more?" Elijah raised to his knees, and placing the back of his right hand in the palm of his left had cried, "I beg of you! I beg of you! I beg of you!" I told the big policeman that that was enough. As we went into the police station where they put Elijah into a cell and locked him up, the Chief of Police again assured me that Elijah would receive ample punishment. In fact, he said, "He will most likely spend twenty years in prison in hard labor." He went on to explain that Elijah had shamed the entire Ashanti people. I was a guest in their city, and what Elijah did was a disgrace to all of Ghana.

I stood outside of Elijah's jail cell and asked him why he did it. He explained that after he had dusted and swept out the inside of the car, he wondered what the powerful engine would sound like. He decided to start the engine. He then thought to himself, it would do no harm to just take a short drive around the block and come right back. That is what he said he intended to do. He said he would have my car back and I would never know it had been gone. But you can be sure your sins will find you out. He said that as he went around the block, a taxi failed to give him the right away, and he had an accident. The damage to the taxi was only minor, and you could not tell the Comet had been in an accident. It took time to get things sorted out with the taxi driver, and that is why my car was not there for me when I came out of my class.

I protested to the Chief of police that the punishment he had described for the crime was far too severe. He proceeded to tell me that there were very few auto thefts, and that the crime rate in Kumasi was very low. He attributed it to the severe penalties meted out for even the smallest crimes. He said it is a necessary deterrent.

He then handed me a sheet of paper and asked me to formally file a complaint, without which, they could not hold Elijah. I gave a sigh of relief! I informed the Chief that I wanted to drop any charges against Elijah. I told him that I was partly to blame for giving him my keys, and once again, the punishment is far to severe for the crime. The Chief became very angry and told me I was making a big mistake. He went on to say that he had heard of the lawlessness in America, and now understood better why it was so.

As we were getting ready to return to the hotel, Elijah came running out of the police station. He fell on his knees and began kissing my feet, tears pouring down his face, and repeating over and over, "Thank you sir! Thank you sir! Thank you sir.!"

As we drove away from the hotel the next morning on the way back to Accra, I was still rather shaken up over what had happened with Elijah and the Comet. But I also had a sense of satisfaction because I knew I had helped to save a young boy's life. I thought, in a measure, it was a small example of what Jesus does when He forgives us of all of our sins. I John 1:9

I read in a book entitled *Ashanti Religion and Art* by Captain Ratray, that Ahanti laws were very severe. The punishment for adultery, like in The Old Testament was death for both parties involved. However, in Ashanti law it was not death by stoning. The guilty pair was brought before the chief and elders. The man was first emasculated, and then both of them were paraded around, and as they walked, pieces of flesh from their buttox were sliced off and pushed into their face with the question asked, "When is the last time you have seen your behind from the day of your birth?" They then chopped off their heads with a ceremonial sword that was supposed to be so sharp that the victims didn't even feel it. One such victim laughed, after the sword fell on his neck, and taunted, "You missed." The executioner responded, "Shake your head." (Joking again) I can well understand why there is so little adultery in the Akan nation.

I might mention that on the way home, we hit a large chuck hole and broke the back springs on the green Comet. It would have taken at least three months to get new springs from the States, so I had a set made by a Ghanaian black smith. Somehow they were not installed correctly, so from that time on we bounced down the road.

When we arrived back in Tesano, I found Christian Adjei, with his father and mother, in our living room talking to Normadeene. Christian had come to enroll in Ghana Christian College! It was not long before the teaching in the class room convinced Christian Adjei that Jesus was in deed the Christ, the Son of the Living God. One afternoon, Cyril Simkins, Richard Hostetter and myself took Christian down to the ocean and carried him out into the ocean, and buried him in the watery grave of Christian baptism. This was the very same ocean that many of his ancestors were carried away from Africa to become slaves in America. Christian was being freed from a slavery far more deadly than his ancestors endured. For the Scriptures ask, "Don't you know that to who you yield yourselves slaves to obey, his slave you are to who you obey, whether it be sin unto death or obedience unto righteousness." Romans 6:16. Christian chose the latter. His choice had a profound effect on his own future as well as the future of Ghana Christian College as I will share with you later.

Not long after, we started our classes in full swing. We had twenty-two regular students, and later added about thirty part time students who attended evening classes. Many of our part time students walked for miles to get to the college. Our student did have a *tremendous hunger for the truth,* as suggested by Max Ward Randall when he toured Ghana for the first time.

Shortly after we started our classes, there was an attempted coup to overthrow the government of Ghana. General Ankrah was the President at that time. The coup failed, but unfortunately, and tragically for the people of Ghana, Major General Kotoka was killed during the attack on Flagstaff

House and Christiansborg Castle. The whole nation went into mourning on word of his death. This was the first time we really felt close to the Ghanaian people as a whole. We mourned with them. We attended the funeral celebration at Black Star Square. Everyone was carrying something that was blood red, the symbol of death by an enemy. It was very much like what the American people experienced after the assassination of John F. Kennedy.

That very same day we received a telegram from Edgar and Mabel Nichols telling us they would be arriving in Accra the next morning. We were excited over their coming, because we knew what it would mean to Chief Mensah and the people of Afancho, who needed the clinic they were to establish, so badly. Their arrival would also take away a little of the sting of Major General Kotaka's death.

Christian Adjei, Principal of Ghana
Christian College with wife and son

Chapter XVIII

THE ANGEL AND A KING

(The Nichols arrive in Ghana)

The day came when Edgar and Mabel Nichols were to arrive on the soil of Ghana. As we suggested earlier, an attempted coup resulted in the death of one of the national heroes of Ghana, Major General Kotaka. Also, as suggested earlier, it was a time of national mourning. People would run through the streets of Accra dressed in red, or waving red handkerchiefs.

Due to the instability that resulted from Major General Kotak's death, security was tightened all over the country. When I arrived at the airport with John Addu, our business manager, we were met by several big, burly security officers, and told that only one of us would be allowed to enter the airport terminal. John Addu was sure he would have to stay outside, and that I would go into the terminal to greet the Nichols. Even though I was very eager to do so, I deemed it important to allow John Addu to carry out his duties. He could understood the language and the procedures necessary for entering Ghana. He proved to be very valuable, in months to come in this respect. John proudly strutted past the security guards into the terminal. I stood by outside, feeling sorry for myself, as I was very anxious to welcome our friends from America with a warm greeting and hug.

As I stood there, a well dressed African man walked up to me and said, "Come with me." I followed him past the security guards, who seemed to not even see us, into the V.I.P. lounge. I turned to thank the man, but he was gone. I know now that that well dressed African man who led me by the security guards was my angel! Just then, I looked, and there stood a man dressed in the regalia of an African king. He spotted me, and inquired in a loud voice, "Who are you?" I looked back at him and asked, "Who are you?" He replied, "I am Offori Atta II, the Omanhene of Kibi." I immediately realized I was addressing one of the most powerful kings in Ghana. He inquired of me again, "Who are you?" I replied, "I am Jerry Gibson of Ghana Christian College and Minnesota Bible College in America. To my dismay, he began to exclaim in that same loud voice, "God is wonderful! God is wonderful! God is wonderful! I have been praying I would meet you, and God has sent you to me!" He went on to explain to me that his nephew, Eric Danquah had told him about my mission to Ghana, and he was eager to meet me, and that God brought me to him that day. That is when I first realized it was my angel that led me past the security guards, into the Omenhene's presence in the V.I.P. lounge.

I started putting things together. Several weeks earlier, I heard a knocking on my door at the Wycliff Translator's house. Two well dressed African men stood there. One of them was Offori Atta's nephew, Eric Donqua. He had recently been released from Nsawam Prison, where he had been confined for five years as a political prisoner, during the Nkruma regime. His uncle, the famous educator, Joseph

Donqua had died during that time in Nsawam Prison. Eric's wife thought he was dead and remarried. Eric explained to me that while he was in prison, he realized that the only thing really important in this life is one's relationship to God, through His Son, Jesus Christ. He said he had heard of our mission to establish a college to train African ministers and evangelists, and was offering his services to me. The man with him agreed to do the same. He had told his uncle, Offori Atta II about our mission. God heard his prayers in regard to meeting me, and God's angel brought us together at the airport. Needless to say, it was a great joy to finally meet with Edgar and Mabel Nichols. It was also a great confirmation of the fact that *man proposes, but it is God who disposes.* God used the arrival of the Nichols in Ghana to answer the king's prayers.

Offori Atta was there to greet his son whom he had not seen for five years. His son had just received his law degree in England, and now with Nkrumah gone, could return home and practice law in his native land. I watched the two of them embrace and snapped a picture. I saw the tears of joy flow freely from the eyes of that father and son. It was a foretaste of what I believe it will be like in heaven when loved ones are reunited. He then turned to me and said, "Please be at my palace in Kibi by 10:A.M. on Monday morning. I have some very important business to discuss with you." I replied, "I will be there." Considering the way we met, I felt I had no choice in the matter.

Early on Monday morning we boarded the V.W. Combi buss that Richard Hostetter had brought with him from Northern Rhodesia. Cyril Simkins joined us for the journey to Kibi The two of them agreed to accompany me to Kibi after I had shared with them the strange circumstance of our meeting. The road between Accra and Kibi was much like driving on a mountain railway. We soon learned that we should drive by faith and not by sight, on roads that seemed impassable. We finally arrived in Kibi at about 10: A.M. We drove directly to the king's palace. Standing in front of the gate were two large guards. We told them who we were. They told us that they were expecting us. They went on to tell us that the king was waiting for us in the Parliament Building. The British had ruled Ghana for the first half of the Twentieth Century. When they left in 1957, The Ghanaians took over the buildings, and continued to conduct government business there.

As we approached the Parliament Building, we noticed that there were no people in sight. We got out of the VW bus and proceeded to walk up a flight of stairs that led to the only entrance we could see into the building. We walked down a long hall and opened the door at the end of the hall. To our dismay, there sat more than one hundred African chiefs and linguists, dressed in their beautiful colored Kente cloths, and their linguists, with their golden linguist staffs. I was frightened. I asked myself, "How do I get into situations like this?" As we stepped into the room, we were greeted by, "Aquaba" to which we responded, "Madassi Pe." They welcomed us, and we thanked them. We shook hands with over one hundred African chiefs and their linguists. We proceeded to the middle of the room, and there sitting on his throne, dressed in a beautiful white robe, with a crown on his head that had a golden cross on it, was Offori Atta II, the king that my Angel wanted me to meet.

The king left his throne and ran to me, and embraced me with a warm hug, exclaiming, "God is wonderful! God is wonderful for bringing you here today!" It was a magnificent sight to behold.

After returning to his throne, protocol demanded that he speak to me through an interpreter, even though he could speak perfect English, having a Doctoral Degree from Oxford in England. There was also the usual minimum suo, drink for the weary traveler that had to be either drank, or poured on the ground for the ancestors. Offori Atta II asked me, "What is your mission?", which was always the first question asked. I proceeded to introduce my two companions Cyril Simkins and Richard Hostetter, and then went on to tell them that we had come to Ghana to establish a college for the training of African missionaries and evangelists who could reach their own people with the Gospel of Jesus Christ. We learned that along with the heads of the various tribes represented there that day, news paper reporters had come from Accra, along with various government officials and other dignitaries.

When I finished my presentation, Offori Atta II stood up and delivered a stirring message to those who were present that day. He quoted scriptures such as Proverbs 14:34, "Righteousness exalteth a nation, but sin is an abomination," He concluded his message with words that are still ringing in my ears. He said, "Without Jesus Christ we can do nothing!" He repeated several times the words, "Without Jesus Christ we can do nothing!" I thought, as he electrified the assembly hall with those words, that this was a message The United Nations, or the Congress of The United States has yet to learn.

Before leaving Minnesota Bible College to begin our campus ministry in Illinois, the girls from the college gave Normadeene and me a large, beautiful picture of The United Nations Building, with Jesus on the outside, looking in. That great African king realized what many of the people in high places in our own government have yet to learn. There can be no lasting peace, without the Prince of Peace, Jesus Christ.

Offori Atta II then proceeded to offer me an entire college campus, building and all, if I would establish a school in his village that would make the principles in the Bible central in its teaching. The government had been trying to obtain that property for years, but the king had refused to sell it, as he had a strong desire that the youth of Ghana have an opportunity for a Christian education.

After a delicious meal in Offori Atta II's palace, which included Mampam, the giant lizard John Addu tried to capture, we were taken on a tour of the campus. Offori Atta II led the way in a fleet of Mercedes-Benz automobiles.

We promised the king we would try to help him fulfill his dream for a Christian College. However, as time went by, we found it impossible to staff the college, as not many are willing to leave the comforts and conveniences of their home land to go to a place like Ghana, West Africa to serve the Lord so far away from home. We are confident that the Lord's angel delivered me past the guards at the airport in Accra, so we would have the opportunity to hear Offori Atta II proclaim to the chiefs and other dignitaries, "Without Jesus Christ, we can do nothing!"

Edgar and Mabel arriving in Ghana

Cyril Simkins, Bros Sampong,
with the Nichols after they arrived in
Ghana

Offori Atta II, the King who the angel
brought to Jerry Gibson at the airport

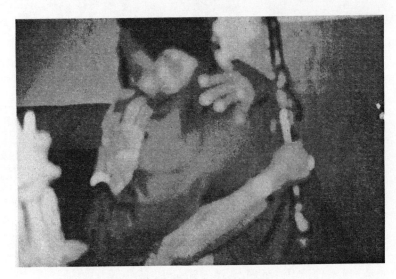

Offori Atta II greeting his son who had been
in exile in the UK for five years

Ghanain dignitaries at the meeting
with Offori Atta II

Offori Atta II with his Mercedes on the
campus offered to Jerry

Jerry Gibson on the throne
with Offori Atta II King of Kibi

Chapter *XIX*

THE ALBERT MENSAH STORY

"That they all may be one"
John 17:22"

"I will cause a thing to happen in your life
time that you will have to see to believe."
Habakkuk 1:5

One of the greatest desires in my heart through the years, is my desire to see Jesus' prayer for the unity of His people answered. After more than two thousand years, Jesus only recorded complete prayer of John seventeen has not yet been answered. The prayer we usually call *The Lord's prayer* should more rightly be referred to as *The Disciples Prayer*." That is what I would like to have happen in my life time. Yes, indeed, I will have to see it to believe it.

I am confident that: (1) It is a *possible prayer*. Jesus would not pray for something that is impossible. It was demonstrated in the first chapter of the Book of Acts. Acts 4:32 says, "They had everything in common." (2 It is a *desirable prayer*. Can you imagine what it would be like to have no need for names on our church buildings. There would be no need to ask, "What church do you belong to, etc., etc." Just for Jesus' sake would be a great blessing. (3) It is an *absolutely necessary prayer* because there is no salvation outside of the one body of Christ. John 14:6; Acts 4:12. I mention this due to what I am about to share with you.

One of our first students at Ghana Christian College was Brother Kuevi. We refer to him as Kuevi. Kuevi brought Brother Nartey to sit in on my classes. Brother Nartey was from Tamali in the Northern Territory of Ghana. I was expounding on Jesus' prayer for unity mentioned above. I presented the three above propositions and went on t o explain to the class that I was a part of a movement whose plea was for the unity of all of God's people. We refer to it as "The Restoration Movement." I told them that we believe that the church established in the days of the Apostles was the perfect pattern for the church of all ages. Our plea and desire was to restore the church after that pattern.

I went on to explain that if we had listened to the Apostle Paul's admonition in I Corinthians 2:1-5, and especially verses four and five, we could have covered a multitude of sins, and we would have the unity Jesus prayed for. The great apostle said, "And my message and my preaching were not in persuasive words of wisdom, but of demonstration of the Spirit and of power, that your faith should not rest on the wisdom of men, but on the power of God." I continued by telling them that if people would investigate their faulty opinions, denominationalism would fall. People often do not understand that the conscience is not an informer, but an accuser. The intellect informs, and the conscience accuses. Therefore, if our thinking is wrong, our conscience will also be wrong. I told them we must get back to a proper "dividing the word of truth" in the Bible. II Timothy 2:15. The Apostle Paul was warning us against following theology that is based on the blending of biblical teaching and the wisdom of men. The Bible and the Bible alone will make not the only Christians, but Christians only.

When we closed the class, Brother Nartey rushed to the front of my class room and introduced himself to me. He said he was on the staff of The University of Northern Ghana in Tamali. He went on to say that in his town there were churches from almost every Christian denomination, as well as Buddhists and Muslims. He said that he was convinced, after hearing my lecture, that if I would accept an invitation to give that same lecture in the Assembly Hall of his university, most of the denominations would want to do away with the denominational barriers that separated them from the other denominations, and help to answer Jesus' prayer for the unity of His people.

Cyril Simkins and Richard Hostetter had not yet arrived in Ghana, so I told Brother Nartey that as soon as they were here and settled in, I would bring them with me, as I wanted them to be able to follow up whatever we accomplished, after I was back in the States. He was excited at the prospect of our coming to Tamali and waited for my reply.

Early one Saturday morning, Cyril Simkins, Richard Hostetter and myself, waved goodbye to our wives as they saw us off, as we boarded a Ghana Airways airplane, that, incidentally, you fly by faith and not by sight. Yes, back in 1966 the old C-47 *goonie bird* airplane, as we named them, a converted U.S. Airforce cargo plane, left much to be desired in comparison to our commercial airliners today.

It was an interesting and rather exciting journey from Accra to Tamali. As we winged our way over the Accra plain, we saw that part of Ghana from a different perspective. The houses for the most part were modern in design, and the University of Ghana as well as Black Star Square and *Job* Six *Hundred* stood out as a stark reminder of what had transpired in Ghana during the regime of Kwami Nkrumah. It has been estimated that Dictator Nkrumah had squandered some six hundred million pounds of Ghanain money into the building of *JOB Six Hundred*, a large multistoried high rise that was supposed to house The organization of African States, in an effort to unite the various countries of Africa, but never came to fruition.

As we traveled further north, the landscape changed, and instead of the modern houses of the Gold Coast with its tropical, palm tree covered coast line, we started to see rectangular shaped houses, with shiny tin roofs, in small villages surrounded by gigantic cotton wood trees that rose up into the sky like our giant redwoods in California. As we flew further north, we flew over the Rain Forest where more than two hundred inches of rain falls each year, most of it during the few months of *the rainy* season. Then, as we flew further north, the landscape changed drastically. We could see signs of the Sahara Desert creeping its way south from Mali and Timbuktu. The land was barren of trees and the houses were no longer rectangular shaped with tin roofs, but were round shaped grass huts with thatched roofs.

I will never forget the thrill we received when we found ourselves circling the airport in Tamali. There was a large sign painted in the cement runway with the words *TAMALI*. When our plane taxied to a stop, we reminded one another that this was the first time American missionaries had landed on that soil with the mission we had come to accomplish. It gave us goose pimples on our skin and butterflies in our stomachs. Cyril and Richard suggested that I should have the pleasure and the honor of being the first man, with a mission such as ours, to set his feet on the soil of Tamali, because I was the one who was invited to speak at the university. I yielded to their suggestion, and to this day, I still feel the surge of excitement that enveloped my being that moment when my feet touched that cement runway.

Brother Nartey and his friend, Brother Jumah, met us at the airport in Brother Jumah's Peugot 404, which proved to be the most reliable vehicle for the unimproved roads of Ghana. We were using their automobile and their petrol. We made it a point to do nothing for the Africans that they could better do for themselves. In the words of the late J. F. Kennedy, we taught them to think, "Not what the white missionary can for us, but what can we do for the white missionary?" Unfortunately, most missionaries, and even our government, have not learned that lesson. People do not appreciate what they get for nothing. If it doesn't cost anything, it is not work anything. The gift that counts is the gift that costs. *There is a lot of might in the mite!* Contrary to what you may have been told, the best things in life are not free! The most costly transaction ever made was the death of Jesus Christ on a cross outside of Jerusalem in 30A.D. Acts 20:28

Brother Jumah and Nartey loaded our luggage in the trunk of the Peugo and drove us to the campus of The University of Northern Ghana. They took us to a small dormitory room which had only two small cots for the three of us. We pushed them together and Cyril and I slept on the outside and let the younger of us, Richard Hostetter sleep in the middle.

The Africans try to do only one important thing each day. The order of business for that Saturday afternoon was for us to visit the leaders of all of the churches in Tamali and give them a special invitation to come to the university on Sunday morning to hear my lecture. We visited every church's minister as well as the leaders from other religious groups. As we approached the last of the ministers we were supposed to invite to Sunday's meeting, both Jumah and Nartey stressed the fact that this man was the most important we would visit. They said it was imperative that he be there if our mission was to be a success. They were speaking of Father Albert Mensah, a charasmatic priest of the Anglican Church, the number one church in Ghana. He had the pleasure of hosting the Queen of England after the British had given Ghana its independence in 1957. They told us that how he responded would influence all of the others.

We approached Albert Mensah's compound and were met by his charming wife Katherine. She welcomed us into her home and informed us that Father Mensah was taking a shower. We spoke to him through the shower curtain. He immediately started to make excuses for why he could not accept our invitation. He finished with the excuse that he had a Mass and six o'clock and another at ten o'clock. I countered by telling him that my lecture would be at eight o'clock, and promised I would try to be done in time for him to make his second Mass. He did not give any assurance that he would be there. As we walked to the car, Jumah and Nartey complained that our mission would fail because Albert Mensah would not be there. I thought to myself, if God wants him to be there, he will be there. He did not bring us all of the way here for our mission to fail. As I have often remarked, "Man proposes, but it is God who disposes."

A little before 8:00 A.M. we arrived at the Assembly Hall. As we entered the building, to my delight, and surprise, the entire audience rose to their feet, in a gesture of welcome respect. We were ushered to the front of the auditorium, and there, sitting on the front row, dressed in his priestly garb, was Albert Mensah. He had rushed from his first Mass to hear my lecture. I was praising God as I stepped to the podium, after having been introduced by Brother Jumah, and welcomed by a rousing round of applause. As I approached the lectern., I prayed the prayer of the boy who fell into the molasses barrel, "Dear Lord, please make my mouth up to this occasion."

After introducing Cyril Simkins and Richard Hostetter, whose value to our mission can not be over emphasized, I began my lecture by telling them how Samuel Clemens, better known as Mark Twain, once said, "Everybody talks about the weather, but nobody ever does anything about it." I went on to say that in regard to Christian unity, the same is true. Everybody talks about it, but very few are willing to do anything about it. I continued by telling them that I had come to share with them a plan that would unite a divided church and answer Jesus' unanswered prayer for the unity of His people. The outline of my sermon was as follows :

    I.   Jesus' word must have absolute authority in all matters of faith and practice. (Matthew 28:17; John 12:48; Colossians 1:18.)

    II.   There must not be any semblance of compromise with Jesus word. Where

Jesus has spoken we don't ask questions, we just obey.

III We must recognize that the Church is not an institution of human origin. Jesus said, "I will build my church." Jesus is the head of His church and the head controls the body. I Corinthians 12:12; Colossians 1:18. Peter is not the "Rock". Jesus is the "Rock", Acts 4:12 and 1 Corinthians 10:4.

IV. We must recognize that the Bible is not a mere book, but it is the very mind of God revealed to man. (II Timothy 3:16,17; II Peter 1:21)

V. Human creeds, human dogmas, human articles of faith, human disciplines, as well as anything human, must not be placed on an equal level of authority with God's word. (I thought of the 39 Articles of the Anglican Church)

VI. We must follow the practices outlined in the New Testament for conducting the business of the church. Jesus told His disciples to "teach all things." Matthew 28:20. We believe they did and what they taught is sufficient.

VII. We must have a genuine love one for another. Colossians 3:14 admonishes, "Beyond all of this, put on love which is the perfect bond of unity."

I concluded by urging them to take special note of John 13:34 and 35 which tells us we must lead by example. "They will know we are Christians by our love for each other. The Romans in the First Century,

even though they did not embrace Christianity,
commented on the Christian community, "Oh, how
they loved each other!"

I then invited any in the audience who wanted
to be a part of a movement to answer Jesus
unanswered prayer for the unity of His people to
respond by walking to the front of the auditorium.
The response was overwhelming. Better than half
of those present rushed to the front to make their
commitment to my invitation. We later took a
picture in front of the Assembly Hall of many of
those who responded that morning. To them Jesus
prayer was possible.

Just before I left the podium, Albert Mensah
came forward and handed me a, note and then
left for his second Mass. We were given a standing
ovation from the crowd. Then I nervously opened
Albert Mensah's hurriedly scribbled note. It said,
"I would like to see you in by bungalow this
afternoon." Nartey and Jumah were sure that I
had somehow offended him.

That afternoon, we once again pulled up to Albert
Mensah's compound. He saw us coming and didn't
wait for us to get out the car. He came running out,
with a large smile on his face, proclaiming,
"Professor Gibson, you have made my day! You have
made my day! You have made my day! For years my
head has been full, but my heart has been empty.
Today you brought joy into my heart. I want to be a
part of the movement that will help to answer Jesus'
prayer for the unity of His people". It was a time of
rejoicing for us all. Once again, this is proof that
Jesus did not pray an impossible prayer. Several
years later in Liberia, four hundred Liberian
ministers and educators made the same response

unanimously to the same message. Yes indeed, Jesus'valuable prayer can be answered in my life time.

We were to fly back to Accra that evening, but when we arrived at the airport, we found that we had been "bumped" from our seats. Somebody had "dashed" the ticket agent and he had given them our seats on the plane

We spent a sleepless night in the airport. We knew our wives would be very worried and wonder what happened to us. However we managed to get a message to them and explain our dilemma.

I might mention, that while I was waiting at the airport, I spied an interesting bundle of twisted wires in the show case of a gift shop. I asked if it was for sale. The sales person said he did not know what it was, but would sell it to me for three cedis. I quickly produced three cedis and proceeded to stuff it into my suit case. I had purchased a bundle of one the oldest forms of monetary exchange. Each twist on the wire represented so many sheep, goats or other valuable consumer goods. I have that bundle of "ancient money" on display in my living room along with other treasures we brought back with us from Africa. As we took off from the airport the next morning, I knew that Father Albert Mensah would have an important roll to play in our lives for many years to come.

Albert Mensah with friend in Chicago

Albert Mensah with Bob Judd and Jack
Rampelberg in Chicago

Chapter XX

JAIL BIRDS AND OUR PARROT

We conducted worship services on the college campus each Lord's Day. For the most part, the students orchestrated the order of worship and provided the music. Cyril Simkins, Richard Hostetter and I did the preaching. On one Sunday morning we arrived to find the students in a minor uproar, little ready for a meaningful worship service. Upon inquiring, we found that there had been a fight the night before. John Addu had *locked horns*, so to speak, with one of the other students. From what we understood, the two men became so angry that they tried to kill each other. To avoid a tragedy, another student contacted the police at the Nima station. Our good friend, Chief of Police Agbete, responded to the call. I inquired of the students as to the whereabouts of John Addu and his adversary. I was told they were in jail at the Nima police station.

I drove to the police station and was met by my good friend Chief Agbete. He explained the situation, but had not yet filed any charges as he wanted to save our college as much embarrassment as possible. I apologized to the chief and thanked him for his gesture of concern and friendship. I assured him this would not happen again. He agreed to release John Addu and the other student into my custody. I paid a small fine, and then took the two men back to the college with me. Both of them were *model students* the rest of the school year.

A week later we returned for the worship service and found a very pleasant, worshipful atmosphere. As we closed the services, we walked out of the building and saw John Addu walking towards us with something on his head. It turned out to be a bird cage. John had climbed up a tree and captured a young West African Gray Parrot. He brought it as a gift for our family, and also as a partial atonement for the stress he had caused us a week earlier. The West African Gray is the most sought after of all parrots. They are the best talkers and live to a ripe old age. The children loved him, and Roland soon became his friend. We named him "Preacher" because he sang, "You are going to reap whatever you sew," which he learned from a song that was very popular with our students. They would break out into joyous singing of that song whenever the spirit moved them. "Preacher" spent much of his leisure time singing that song.

Every time we saw or heard "Preacher" singing, we were reminded of the Sunday morning we had to get our *jail bird* students out of jail.

Not long after that incident, and not long after the Hostetters arrived in Ghana with their three children, Steve, Jeff and Heather, another occasion stands out vividly in our minds. We had cautioned our children about the danger of getting off of the beaten paths, and the necessity of staying on the main roads. Snakes, scorpions, and other poisonous creatures were everywhere. That was especially true of vacant lots. Also, there were giant ant hills, that housed ants that we were told were also poisonous. They stood like giant red pillars all over the Ghanaian countryside. We cautioned the children to stay clear of them, also, as we were told that a sting from one of those ants could also be lethal. However, unfortunately, children do not always obey their parent's wishes. The Hostetter boys had walked from their house to our house to escort Becky back to their house so they could play together. Instead of doing as we had asked, the boys decided to take a short cut across a vacant lot. Becky followed the boys. Their route took them past several large red ant hills. We heard a scream! We ran out of the house and looked across the street to the vacant lot. There, standing on an ant hill, was Becky, covered from head to toe with giant ants. One sting could be deadly for her. We were helpless. All we could do was pray. God heard our prayer and sent our angel. In a moment the ants were off of her body. She did not have a single sting! We rebuked her and the boys soundly! We both laughed and cried. Once again, our angel had saved Becky.

There were also plenty of fun times.

Ghana is a beautiful country, and outside of its location and sometimes climate, as well as some unfriendly bugs and mosquitoes, it may be considered a paradise for tourism. I suggested the same to several travel agents when we returned home from Ghana.

It was only a few miles from our home to one of the most beautiful beaches in the world. We would load our children and Roland, who loved the ocean, into our car, and head for the beach. We did not have to pack a lunch because enterprising Ghanaians had set up small vending bars all along the beach. The Cape Coast road took us by wonderful and intriguing sights. On the beach at Winneba, Becky had her own private swimming pools. Further on, toward Takorodi was Elmina, with its infamous Elmina Castle. Thousands of African men, women and children were housed there in chains while waiting to be shipped to America and the West Indies to be sold on the auction block as slaves. It has not changed. The chains and holding cells are still there, a stark reminder of the inhumanity of man to man. Fortunately, There are no longer any human beings for sale. Cape Coast was also a very interesting town to visit, full of history.

There were also many very fine restaurants in Accra. Our dear friend, Mr. Matani and his son, Lal, often entertained us in their home. Mr. Matani would hire the chef and his cooking staff from the Maharaja Indian restaurant to come to his home and prepare special Indian cuisine for us. We often ate delicious meals at the Ambassador and Continental hotels in Accra. Due the British ownership of the Ambassador Hotel, we were greeted by a host with proper English greetings and escorted to a table adorned with the finest white linen table cloth and fine China surrounded by exquisite silverware.

I mentioned earlier how Mr. Matani and his son Lal proved to be valued friends. Two incidents really high light their contribution to our mission in Ghana. One had to do with a "bounced" check. The other had to do with helping to make a wedding possible.

The Hindu and the Christians

I can not emphasize enough the value of the Matani's friendship. On one occasion, I had a five hundred dollar check returned for insufficient funds. In Ghana, at that time, I don't know what they do now, when a check bounces, they didn't charge you an overdrawn fee on a little pink slip, they put you in jail! I don't like to go to jail, especially in Africa. I was in jail in Nigeria in 1973. I traveled there with my oldest son, Albert Joseph and a young university student, Dennis Daisey, It was right after the Biafran War. Unfortunately, the U.S. took the wrong side and was very unpopular at the time with the government of Nigeria. We had hosted a Nigerian man named Owu, who was at the University of Illinois getting his doctors degree in physical education. He had a great desire for us to meet his wife and also bring her some things she could not get in Nigeria. I had been corresponding with a man named Uddo. He was a eager for me to establish a Christian college in Nigeria similar to Ghana Christian College. I applied for visas to Nigeria when I applied for our visas to Ghana and Liberia. We planned on spending time in each of these West African countries. We received our visas from the first two countries without any questions, but were flatly refused a visa to enter Nigeria.

I mentioned earlier that Albert Mensah would continue to play a major role in our lives. That proved to be doubly true at this time. When we arrived in Ghana, Katherine, Albert's wife, was there visiting her family. I was enjoying a delicious Ghanaian meal in the home one of the important barristers of Ghana. In the course of our conversation, the subject of our not being able to get visas from Nigeria came up. He informed me that he had a friend in the Nigerian embassy who owed him a favor. He immediately got on the telephone and gave this man a call. He explained the situation to his friend. When he hung up the telephone, he said his friend would be waiting for me and would assist me in getting the necessary visas for Albert Joseph, Dennis and myself.

We left immediately, because time was of an essence, as we would have to arrange for air travel and for someone to meet us at the airport in Lagos, Nigeria. When we arrived at the embassy, we were cordially greeted and handed seven documents to be filled out in triplicate. It was a long and arduous task that awaited us as it took several hours to complete those forms. After spending the remainder of the work day in the Nigerian embassy, we were finally given our visas to enter Nigeria.

Before leaving the States, I had contacted the President of the Bank of Nigeria, a very good friend of Owu. He had corresponded with me and expressed his desire to host us when we came to Nigeria. Before leaving Ghana, I sent a wire to him asking him to meet us at the airport in Lagos. I was eager to meet him and knew he would be of great assistance in helping us accomplish our mission in Nigeria.

As we entered through the security gate, Albert and Dennis were in different lines than me. When the security agent looked at my visa, he immediately called another man who also looked at my visa. That man began to shout at me in both English and Nigerian! He wanted to know how I had obtained a visa when Nigeria was not granting visas to Americans? He then accused me of being a spy! Several men, dressed in black uniforms grabbed me and started dragging me down a hallway. They stopped in front of a jail cell, unlocked the door and pushed me in. I thought that it must have been some kind of night mare and was not really happening. I began to pray. I prayed, "Dear Lord, you helped me get into this country, now dear Lord help me get out!" I had no idea what had happened to Albert and Dennis. I later found out that they were allowed through the security gate without any hassle. To this day, I wonder why?

After I got settled into my cell, one of the guards continued screaming at me. It was mostly in some kind of Nigerian tongue, so I had no idea why he was shouting. Then, a well dressed Nigerian man entered my cell and began to interrogate me. He wanted to know specifically how I managed to get a visa to Nigeria when Nigeria was not granting visas to Americans. I simply told him the truth. I assured him I was not a spy, and told him of my connection with Owu and also mentioned that the President of the Bank of Nigeria in Lagos was supposed to have been there at the airport to meet me. I suggested that they send a wire to the Nigerian embassy in Ghana to corroborate my story. Several hours later, a very sheepish looking Head of Security came back to my cell and began to apologize for any inconvenience I may have been caused and ushered me back out into the main terminal of the airport where I found a very frightened and worried Albert and Dennis. They had no idea what had happened to me. I might mention, that while I was being ushered back into the main airport terminal, the guard who had shouted at me, whispered in my ear, "I did not mean anything I said to you. I was just trying to impress my superiors." He went on to tell me that there were others who wanted his job, and he thought he was pleasing his boss.

We later found out that the President of the Bank of Nigeria had gotten stuck in a traffic jam on the way to the airport and had no idea what had happened to us. The circumstances for us finding that out, as well as the time we spent in Nigeria is a story that needs to be told all by itself in one of my future books.

Back to my situation with the bounced check in Ghana. As you can see from what I just shared with you, I had a strong desire to stay out of jail, and especially in Africa. I immediately went to several Christian missionaries and asked if they could help with a loan until I could contact my Forewording Agent to deposit money in our bank account. The reply I got from them was, "We will pray for you in jail Brother Gibson." As a last resort I went to my Hindu friend, Mr. Matani. I told him of my plight. Without hesitation, he went to his back room and came out with a small tin box. He opened it and proceeded to pick out five one hundred dollar bills and handed them to me without any questions. I thought at the time, "Which of these would be more acceptable to God. The praying Christians or the *giving* Hindu?" I know what conclusion I came to. As I have often said, "It is *possible* to give without loving, but it is *impossible* to love without giving." God taught us that with the death of His son on a cross outside of Jerusalem. John 3:16 By the way, this all happened before the Simkins and Hostetters joined us in Ghana. They would have gladly loaned me the money I needed to stay out of jail.

The most enjoyable and fun time we had each day was going to get our mail. Our mail box was in down town Accra, across from the Market Place. We would all pile into the little green comet and wend our way down town, through the traffic circles to get our mail. We had a postal box with a well worn lock, so it took some maneuvering to get it open. Normadeene and the children were eagerly watching. I reached into the mail box and found one letter. It was from the Junior High class of the Christian Church in Floressant, Missouri. It was written by one of the little girls who was a member of that class. She explained how they heard my presentation about our mission to Ghana when I spoke at her church. She said the teacher and members of her class were very impressed by what they had heard about our mission to establish a college in Ghana. She went on to say that their Sunday school teacher had taught them the importance of being good stewards of their money, and specifically their obligation and the importance of supporting missionaries like myself.

As I have often suggested that, a missionary is one who goes where he has not been, to do what he has not done, with money he does not have. I heard that from a missionary who spoke some years ago at the National Missionary Convention in Louisville, Kentucky. We decided to raise our support in smaller increments. We needed about seven hundred and fifty dollars a month for what we called our "Living Link". We decided to recruit "Lieutenants for Christ" who would give at least seven dollars and fifty cents per month to our mission. That way, if we had one hundred lieutenants, we would have our living link support raised.

The little girl went on to say, "We take two offerings in our class every Sunday. One is for the regular Sunday school program. The other is for missions. We do not have enough each Sunday to be Lieutenants. But could you use a few Corporals?" Included in the letter was a check for forty dollars. Words can not express what a lift this gave to our spirits. When we returned home, I held the first of seven Faith Promise Missionary week ends with the Florissant Church. In the front pew sat most of the students and the teacher from that class of "Corporals for Christ." Their faces were beaming for the joy of having a part in establishing Ghana Christian College and Seminary which today is approaching its Fortieth Anniversary and has trained hundreds of specialized Christian servants, and is soon to be in a new college campus.

Elmina Castle where many African slaves
were housed before being shipped to the
West Indies and America

Ghanaian Policemen at
Ghana International School

Chapter XXI

THE WEDDING

One of the most enduring and precious friendships we have experienced in our life time had its beginning while we were in Ghana. We received a letter from a young Peace Corp worker from Holyoke, Colorado, Douglas Keasling. He expressed his desire for me to perform the wedding ceremony for him and another Peace Corp worker, Beth Stroffoleno from Vermont. They were both teachers in a small village west of Kumasi named Dunkwa. They had heard of our work in Ghana through a mutual friend. They desired a Christian minister to officiate at their wedding. I had married The McDonalds while I was still in Kumasi, and I saw no reason for not doing the same for Doug and Beth Keasling. We had no idea what we were getting into. They needed to obtain a wedding license and also find a chapel to be married in, etc. etc. When we went to the Ministries to apply for their wedding license, we were told there was a three months wait from the time the license is issued to the time that actual ceremony takes place. We did not ask why, but immediately started looking for a special dispensation for Doug and Beth. This was Friday and they wanted to be married the next day on Saturday.

I wanted Doug and Beth to meet our good friends, the Matanis. We stopped by their shop early in the afternoon. We were given our usual "mineral" and then we explained to Mr. Matani our problem. He got on his telephone to call a friend in the ministries. He got his friend just as he was leaving for the week end. He explained to him the situation. The friend said he would go back to his office and draw up the necessary papers for Doug and Beth to be married that day. If Mr. Matani's call had been five minutes later, we could not have had the wedding, for there was no other person in the Ministries that had the authority necessary to make Doug and Beth and exception to the rule.

We gave a large sigh of relief when we walked away from the Ministries building with Doug and Beth's wedding certificate in our hands.

We drove down town Accra the next morning to a beautiful church not far from the post office where we got out mail. The building where weddings take place also had to be approved by the government of Ghana. John Addu was there to stand up with Doug and Normadeene stood up with Beth. The exchange of wedding vows was beautiful. We made reservations for Doug and Beth to stay in the new Continental Hotel on the first night of their honeymoon, and then saw them off the next morning to Ivory Coast where they would spend their real honeymoon. As we look back, we believe the wedding might never have taken place when and where it did had it not been for our friend Mr. Matani.

We have stayed in close touch with Doug and Beth Keasling through the years. Doug eventually took his bride back to Holyoke, Colorado with him. Then they moved to Fort Collins where they have lived ever since. They have been on the Board of Directors of World-Wide Missions Outreach from the time of its inception. Doug was the first Chairman of the board. Beth has served faithfully as our secretary. We had the privilege of traveling with them to China in 1993. We have both been able to keep in contact with Chinese friends we met at that time.

Jerry with Lal and Mr. Matani.
Mr. Matani kept Jerry out of jail

G.A., Cindy, Gibby and John Adu with Lal
and Mr. Matani in their store

Normadeen and Jerry
with Doug and Beth Keasling in front
of the church where they were married

Doug and Beth Keasling with Jerry right
after they were married

Chapter XXII

THE AFRICAN TRADERS

One of the most interesting experiences we had while in Ghana was our haggling with Nigerians, as well as other African traders. Almost on a daily basis, we would hear a knocking at our door, or see, as we looked out of our window, an African man or woman with a large bundle of goods on their head, hoping to leave with some of our money in their pockets. They were usually skilled sales persons who knew and practiced the universal outline for marketing. They answered three questions: (1) What is it? (2) What is it worth? And (3) How do you get it?

They would spread out their wares on a blanket or rug and watch us as we looked at the many treasures they had brought with them. They would watch our eyes and somehow could tell if a certain object met our fancy. Then they applied the above principles in order to make a sale.

We became rather close friends to many of them and called them by name. One Nigerian man who we called "Smiley" became a regular visitor to our house. For some reason, our dog Roland did not like the traders. He would bark loud and growl at them. They were afraid of him, so we would have to put him in the house until they left.

We treasure some of the art objects we purchased from the traders. We are including pictures in this book of some of them that are very special to us. There is our ebony Mali heads which was one of the first pieces we acquired. It weighs possibly forty pounds, as ebony is a very solid wood. It comes from deep below the surface of the water in a river or lake. I traded a pretty little gold watch that chimed on the hour that I purchased in Geneva, Switzerland for the Mali head. We also have two large ebony masks hanging on the wall of our family room. We have a "bumbara" which has much religious significance in the African culture. It has the scars of termites on it as it is very old. We have a carved wooden linguist staff and also a large drum in the form of a woman's torso. One of the very unique pieces of art we brought back with us is a "judgment statue". The termites did take a toll on that too. It is a carved statue with a removable carved monkey on the top of its head. We were told that when a man or woman was accused of a capital crime, they would stand before the king or chief who often had extreme powers, even the power of life and death. He would ask the prisoners if they were guilty of the crime. If they said, "No." He would ask them to remove the monkey from the head of the statue. If they were guilty, supposedly the could not. Most of them did not even try.

We have a display case in our living room filled with brass art objects we brought back from Ghana. We believe that today we would not be able to bring back many of our brass art treasures, as they would be considered national treasures and could not be taken out of the county. We have pictures of some of some of these in this book, also.

We have a brass *judgment head* that was used like the judgment statue mentioned above. The only difference is that the king or chief listens to the defense of the prisoner and then decides for himself the guilt or innocence of the accused. He holds the judgment head behind his back with his finger stuck in a hole. If he thinks the accused is guilty, he produces the judgment head, and they are pronounced guilty. We have a *"Kaduo pot* that is a beautiful example of African art. It has carved figures on its side and a removable top with the carved brass figures of a pregnant woman holding a linguist staff. These pots are very unique. They are said to have held the precious and other valuables of their owners.

We also have a number of what are called "gold weights". They are figures carved in brass, from men to various animal forms. Crossed crocodiles are very common. We have examples of many of these art objects in our display cabinet. We have several very old *ju ju pots,* said to be used by witch doctors to prepare their potions. All of these objects seem to have a religious significance. This prompted us to have a special desire to research deeper into their religious back ground. I purchased a book by Captain R.S.Rattray entitled, "Ashanti Religion and Art". It was so interesting to read that I had a hard time putting it down. Unfortunately, I recently loaned it to a friend and he has misplaced it. I am hope I can locate another copy on the internet.

We brought back some beautiful *Kente cloth,* which is peculiar to the Akan culture. A story is woven into the pattern of the cloth. It is very costly, but worth every penny, as it takes hours of painstaking effort to produce a garment.

We should mention here that *haggling* was one of the most important aspects of our dealing with the traders. We usually had a pretty good idea as to what we would be willing to pay for a particular object. We compared what one trader asked for a similar object with what the one we were haggling with was asking for his art object. We would ask, "How much?" He would state a highly inflated price like one hundred cedis. We would respond with a gasp, "Too dear! Too dear!" We would make a counter offer. He would respond, "Debbie Da! Debbie Da!", "No never! No Never!" This went on until both of us were satisfied that we had achieved the law of fair exchange, where both parties believe they have the best of the deal. It was difficult for us to get over the practice of haggling when we returned to America.

Many of the things we got from the traders were things we planned to use on our missionary display table when we got back to America. We gave slide presentations and then spoke about the things on our table. Just before leaving Ghana a trader came by with a twenty-foot plus boa constrictor skin. The large snake had coiled itself around a large pig and squeezed it to death. Then it unhinged its jaws and proceeded to swallow it whole. The trader had killed the boa and retrieved the pig and then tanned its hide. It is beautiful. It is large enough to make many hand bags, belts or sandals. I wanted it because it is the kind of thing that gets the attention of ornery little boys when you are making your missionary presentation. I had a pair of cowboy boots I had brought from America that hurt my feet. I managed to haggle the trader into taking my boots in exchange of his boa constrictor skin. I also purchased a spear and bow and arrow set which did an excellent job of getting the attention of little boys. I will try to get a good picture of the boa constrictor skin and the bow and arrow, along with a sheath of arrows. to include in this book. The arrows are of the poisonous variety.

African Kudo Pots where chiefs
kept their treasure

African Ebony Mali heads

African Ceremonial Drum

Chapter *XXIII*

THE UNIVERSITY OF GHANA

IN LEGON

One of the wisest and most profitable things I did was to enroll in The University of Ghana and take two evening semesters of African Studies. I wanted to learn about the Ghanaian and African culture from the African's mind set, rather than the traditional European missionary point of view. With that understanding, I believed I could adjust the curriculum of the college to meet the needs the Ghanaian people and better equip our graduates to do so.

The University of Ghana is the real *show place* for the country of Ghana. It is much more so than Kwami Nkrumah's infamous "Job Six Hundred" or even Black Star Square. When visitors came to Ghana, we made it a point to take them on a tour of the university campus.

The campus is situated on a hill overlooking the Atlantic Ocean. The buildings are built on stair steps up the hill. They have an Egyptian and Oriental motif. Standing tall in the middle of the stair steps is a large clock tower. It has an observation deck that could be reached by an elevator. We often looked out over the campus and the surrounding area from that clock tower observation deck.

The evening classes that I attended were conducted in a large outdoor amphitheater. There were several hundred students in those classes. I believe I mentioned that I was often the only "white man" in the midst of several hundred black men. I stuck out like a sore thumb. I can still hear them call out, "Ho! Brunie! Ho Brunie! (Ho white man) When I came into the amphitheater. And I responded with, "Ho Bibini!" (Ho black man). I urged the professor to not change his lectures because of my being there, as much of what was said had to do with the influence the white man had on the political, social and economic history of Africa. The Russians had come to help, but brought big, clumsy machines that got bogged down in the jungle terrain of Ghana. It was pointed out that Ghana had the resources to produce ninety percent of her needed consumer products, but due to the fact that the Europeans, mainly the British, left Ghana without building the necessary infrastructure to get their products to market. Because of that, she had to import ninety percent of the needed consumer products which had a disastrous effect of the economy, which had very little foreign exchange to work with. When we arrived in Ghana, as I may have suggested earlier, one cidi was worth one dollar and forty cents in American money. When I last visited Ghana in 1993, one American dollar was worth four hundred cedis. That kind of inflation and devaluation of currency is devastating.

Richard Hostetter attended several classes with me and seemed to enjoy them very much. I did not stay in Ghana long enough to receive a degree, but I was able to put together a series of lecture notes on African Studies that would enable me to teach the subject if I so desired.

I enjoyed spending time in the library and the book store. I brought back many books that were very enlightening to me. I still have many of them in my basement library today.

I often wondered how I found time to attend those classes along with the work of running the college. I realize that I would not have been able to do so without the able assistance of my beloved colleagues, Cyril Simkins and Richard Hostetter.

The University of Ghana was a garden paradise. Everywhere you looked would be beautiful clusters of exotic tropical flowers and groves of palm trees. The grounds were always neat and clean and well kept.

Any Ghanaian who could qualify academically, could attend the university tuition free. Many University of Ghana graduates have come to American to receive their graduate degrees. They seem to do very well in our class rooms. We have hosted several of them and found it to be a delightful and rewarding experience. One of the reasons we have worked with International students on our university campuses through the years was the result of what I experienced as a foreign student in Ghana. Better than fifty percent of all International students in America never see the inside of an American home and therefore never really experience what America is all about. All they know about us is what they read in their news papers or see on their television sets. Therefore, many of them have a distorted idea of what the average American thinks or feels. When they get into our homes, contrary to what they have seen or heard, they find out that we are not a bunch of sex possessed pot heads, but are really very much like them.

Chapter *XXIV*

MISSION ACCOMPLISHED

Our mission to establish a college for the training of African ministers and evangelists who could reach their own people with the message of Christ was pretty much accomplished. There were only a few loose ends we had to take care of. However, we soon found out that it would not be easy to leave the work that God had called us to pioneer. By now, the college was staffed by capable and experienced teachers, such as Cyril Simkins and Richard Hostetter. And there were others such as Ron and Doris Rife, and the Kent Taylor family, Ron and Kent being former students of mine in Minnesota Bible College, who were also well qualified, who had committed themselves to the work of Ghana Christian College and were preparing to join the Ghana Christian College family. So we were now ready to return to America.

We had been away from the Minnesota Bible College class room for two years. I was committed to resume my teaching duties there in the Fall semester. We also had to inform the churches in Ghana and some of the key leaders who were instrumental in helping us come to Ghana. And then there were some of our Muslim friends and Mr. Matani and his son Lal who would find it difficult when they learned we were leaving. It is not easy to say good bye to those who are near and dear to you. The Apostle Paul had this same problem with the Ephesian elders as recorded in Acts 20:28-35.

All in all, we were pretty well satisfied with what God had accomplished through our family and our co-laborers. We were especially grateful for the financial and prayer support we had received from our supporting friends and churches.

Becky with student from the college

First student body of
Ghana Christian College

Richard Hostetter, Jerry Gibson and Cyril
Simkins with business manager John Adu.
This was the first staff of the college.

Jerry with Mintah one of our first students

Jerry Gibson lecturing at
Ghana Christian College

Chapter XXV

MY SANCTIFIED NOSE

One night shortly before we started to pack to return to America, I went to bed feeling rather uneasy, but not knowing why? Have you ever experienced that feeling? I had had a particularly busy day and was dead tired. Fortunately we had a very comfortable bed that we shipped over from Minnesota, and also the large window air conditioner that we told you about earlier. Usually, when I was that tired, the sound of the air conditioner blotted out all other sounds and smells and I would immediately fall fast asleep. However, on this particular night it was different. I could not for the life of me get to sleep. I did not know why, as I could not think of any pressing problem that was facing us. But something was terribly wrong.

I usually could go the entire night without having get up to go to the bathroom. However, this night was different in that respect also. I mentioned how the bed rooms in the Wyclif translators house were lined up in a row down the hall that led to the bathroom. Facing the bedrooms, Gibby and G.A.'s rooms were off to our right. Cindy and Becky were sharing the bedroom just to the left of our room between us and the bathroom. When I walked by their room, I noticed that Becky was not yet asleep. On the way back from the bathroom I peeked into

Becky and Cindy's room and whispered to Becky, "If you can't get to sleep, come and crawl in bed with your mother and me. When you fall asleep I will carry you back to your bed." She responded, "Mama will get mad at me. She doesn't like to have me sleep with you. She said I am too big of a girl now." I told her to come if she changed her mind.

I climbed back in bed, but still could not go to sleep. Suddenly I smelled a strange smell. I jumped out of bed and opened the door from our room between Cindy and Becky's room. What I saw horrified me. We placed mosquito coils on the floor between Cindy and Becky's beds. It was not enough to just have mosquito netting around there beds, as the Malaria mosquito had a way of getting to its victims in spite of the netting. Somehow, Becky's blanket had made contact with the mosquito coil. It served as a wick. Her blanket and netting suddenly exploded into a deadly fire. The smoke was already thick and the girls were both asleep. Becky's bed was already enveloped in flames. Cindy's bed was starting to smolder. Normadeene jumped out of bed and ran into the room with me! We grabbed the girls and pulled them out of the fiery room. They were choking and coughing from the smoke they had inhaled. I then grabbed the burning bed, blankets and all and carried it through the hall and out into the back yard. Normadeene ran to the kitchen and brought back a bucket of water that she threw on Cindy's smoldering bed.

When I came back into the house, both Cindy and Becky started to kiss my nose. If I had not smelled smoke from the burning blanket, they would not have returned home to America with us. They would almost certainly have perished in that flaming inferno. My angel had kept me awake. It did not allow us to be tempted "beyond what we would be able to endure." I Corinthians 10:13. We had that warm feeling once again. But not from the fire. Once again, God had given His angels charge over us. Psalms. 91:11. It's interesting how the number of that verse reminds us of September 11, 2001. We spent the rest of the night on our knees in prayer, praising and thanking God for His protective care. Every now and then Cindy and Becky would kiss my "Sanctified Nose".

Chapter XXVI

ABDULLAH OUR MUSLIM FRIEND

We became very close friends to some of the young men we met while retrieving our mail in down town Accra. One of them was a Muslim man named Abdullah. When we told him we were leaving Ghana to return to America he was very sad. He told us that he wanted us to meet his wife and children before we left. We agreed to do this.

Late one afternoon, we drove to a part of Accra that very few white Christians ever frequented. As I mentioned earlier, about driving through the Muslim part of Ashanti New Town, the night we recruited our first students, it was not considered safe for us to venture there. However, Abdullah assured us that he would give us safe passage to his bungalow and that we should meet him at a certain place, to which we complied. I have to admit it was a scary situation. Once again, I could feel the hair stand up on the back of my neck and Normadeene and I made our way past the charcoal pots and strange smells, feeling a thousand eyes on us, as we followed Abdullah to his home.

It was a very humbling experience for us to see how Abdullah and his wife and children lived. Their home was nothing more than a hole in the wall, with no furniture and just a small curtain to separate the two rooms of their apartment. Abdullah's wife got down on the floor and literally kissed our feet. She had prepared some tea and a small white wafer for us to share with them. We felt a love from those two Muslims and their small child that we seldom ever receive from American Christians, especially if they do not agree with our theological position.

When it came time to leave, I offered a prayer in the name of Jesus to bless our friends and thanked him for their love for us. As a gift they gave us two dozen eggs which for them was like giving us a months salary.

Abdullah led us back to our car. By this time it was evening and it was pitch black. Several men followed us very closely, and I prayed that our angel would walk along side Abdullah until we got back to our car. When we arrived home, Isaac and Benjamin inquired as to where we had been. When we told him we had visited Abdullah's bungalow they had a fit. They said we should never have taken such a chance and were surprised we got out of there alive. They told us of several Europeans who entered that area and were never heard from again. We assured them that there was nothing for them to fear. I quoted Second Timothy 1:7 which tells us, "We have not been given the spirit fear, but of power, love and self control." Also, we knew God's angels were watching over us.

Chapter XXVII

CHRISTMAS IN GHANA

As I look back, another memorable experience comes to mind that I should share with you. Holidays were especially difficult for our family, as they brought pangs of homesickness into our hearts. I recall the first Fourth of July we spent in Ghana. A large number of ex-patriots met in the American Flats area of Accra to celebrate our nations birthday. I missed being at home during the Christmas and other holiday seasons while I was on Guam during the Second World War. However, that was different from what we experienced in Ghana as a family. On Guam, I was surrounded by American servicemen, who like myself were there for a very just cause. In Ghana there were so very few of us, that we felt very much alone. The *powers to be* flew in coca cola and hot dogs from New York City. We stood in line to get a hot dog. It was delicious. An American army officer who was serving as an advisor to the Ghanaian military led us in the Pledge of Allegiance and then attempted to lead us in "The Star Spangled Banner". I said, "attempted", because most of us had throats so tight with the emotion and love for our country that we could not sing a note. At the time I thought of the words of Walter Scott, "Lives there a man with soul so dead, who never to himself has said, this is my own, my native land!"

On Christmas of 1966, Normadeene and Becky
and I traveled to Nkawka to hold special Christmas
eve and Christmas day services. We left Albert and
Cindy home to take care of our animals. They were
well taken care of. Mr. Matani and Lal brought them
to their house for a Christmas Eve dinner. And they
were busy trying to make Christmas decorations in
order to make our home seem a little more like
Christmas.

Normadeene and Becky and I were housed in the
second story of a little hotel in down town Nkawka.
We looked out on to the court yard. We noticed a
little lamb tethered to a small tree. We learned that
it was a "sacrificial lamb" to be ceremonial sacrificed
on Christmas morning in honor of "the lamb of God
who came to take away the sins of the world." John
1:29 Becky cried when she heard about that.

The next morning we conducted special
Christmas services under a compound covered with
palm branches. Before we left to drive back to Accra,
Sarah Samson, one of our students asked if she could
get a ride with us, as she was supposed to be in
class the next day. She was a rather large women.
She sat in the back seat with Becky. I mentioned
earlier that we had broken the back springs of the
Comet on one of our trips to and from Kumasi. Every
time we hit a bump, the body of the car would hit
the frame and make a loud noise. Every time that
happened, Sister Sarah Samson would exclaim, "Oh,
Jesus! Oh, Jesus!" We laughed because we knew
she was not being sac-religious.

When we arrived back home, late that evening,
we had the surprise of our lives. Albert and Cindy
had decorated our living room and dining room with
home made Christmas decorations, and had
decorated an artificial Christmas tree. They also had

prepared a delicious Christmas dinner. We prayed,
sang a couple of Christmas carols and then, sat down
to one of the most memorable and delicious dinners
we have ever enjoyed. We learned from that
experience that the "Christmas spirit" is in no way
hindered by one's geographical location.

Chapter XXVIII

WHAT WE MISS THE MOST

I have often been asked, what was the most difficult thing to leave and what would we miss the most? There are so many things we could list in this area, but the things we would miss the most were mostly connected with people.

I can close my eyes and look out over my class room. There was an aisle between the desks. As I look out over the right side of that room from my perspective, I can see Kuevi and Benjamin Minta in the back row. In front of them I see Kojo and Bediako. In front of them my mind's eye sees Christian Adjei and Paul Addai.

On my right I see Grace Oku and Sarah Samson. In front of them are Nelson and Elijah. In front of them are Nelson and Mr. Woanya. And then in the front road my minds eye sees Benjamin and Isaac.

In connection with this student body, the thing I miss the most was their spontaneous breaking out into joyous song in the middle of my lectures. Grace Amoku had a beautiful voice that echoed through the class room. She would start by chanting, "You are going to reap whatever you sow. You are going to reap whatever you sow. Upon the mountains, down in the Valleys, you are going to reap whatever you sow." The students sang in perfect harmony. They would then break into, "Are you ready if the Lord should come? Are you ready it the Lord should come? In the morning, six O'clock, in the evening five O'clock, are you ready if the Lord should come?"

Outside of the college class room, the time of receiving the Sunday morning offering stands out as one of the things our family would miss and still misses very much. As I mentioned earlier, the women who sat on the opposite side of the sanctuary from the men, would begin the processional and march to the front where a large tub or basin was placed. They would dance forward, waving their beautiful many colored scarves, singing as they danced and placed their offering in the containers provided. The men would then follow them. The scriptures say that "God loves a cheerful giver." II Corinthians 9:7. The word "cheerful" may also be translated, "hilarious". The Ghanaians truly gave that meaning to the word when they brought their offerings to the Lord. We always thought it was rather humorous, because they would count the money. If they did not believe it was as much as it ought to be, the would start all over again.

Browsing in the Market Place was also a memorable experience. But, as with the case of the college, the people we encountered are what we will miss the most. I have returned to Ghana four times since we first left. The first three were without Normadeene. In 1991 I returned to help celebrate The Silver Jubilee which marked the Twenty-fifth Anniversary of the college. That was a memorable experience. However, the most remarkable experience took place in the summer of 2003 when Normadeene and I both returned to a celebration we will long remember. Ghana Christian College was upgraded to the level of a university. Habakkuk 1:5 declares, "I will cause a thing to happen in your lifetime that you will have to see to believe." We experienced the truth of the statement as we viewed the new campus. The words of the Queen of Sheba to Solomon, "The half has not been told," I Kings 10:7, was the reaction Normadeene and I received when we saw the work that God had done through the labors of those who followed us in Africa.

We realize more and more the wisdom and truth in the statement of the Apostle Paul in I Corinthians 3:6. Max Ward Randall, Cyril Simkins and Normadeene and I were planters. Richard and Nancy Hostetter, Kent and Barbara Taylor, Ron and Doris Rife, Dorothy Eunson and David and Barbara Kalb, along with others like Derry and Dona Smaage and the McHenry's watered. But it is God who gave the increase.

There were several loose ends we wanted to take care of before getting packed up to return home to America. The first was to travel back to Kumasi and encourage the leadership of the Ashanti churches to remain faithful after we left. The Apostle Paul's meeting with the Ephesian elders, as I have mentioned before, was a similar situation as ours. He told them he would probably not see them again in the flesh. They wept over that thought.

We had the same experience when we met for the last time on the Lord's day with our beloved brothers and sisters in Christ there in Kumasi. Edgar and Mabel Nichols were there along with Elder Moses Addai and Mary Ajamin, his daughter. We warned them about "grievous wolves entering in" after we left. Acts 20:28ff. And we wept because we knew that would be the last time we would see each other. We have not seen Edgar and Mabel, as Mabel is now with the Lord, and we have not seen Moses Addai or Mary Ajamin, even though I returned to Ghana several times since then.

Then, there was the matter of the mausoleum outside of Kumasi. I could never quite get the thought of not being able to see the treasures Korbina Kessi told me about, covered with more gold than our proverbial Fort Knox, out of my mind. I thought that perhaps, this time, because it may be my last opportunity, I might be able to get a special dispensation, to at least look inside, and take a few pictures while we were in Kumasi. But that did not happen.

Becky with one of the Hostetter boys in her
own private swimming pool by the ocean

Chapter XXIX

THE FAREWELL SPEECH

"They loved us too much"

As I said earlier, our mission to establish a college for the training of African ministers and evangelists who could reach their own people with the gospel message was accomplished. Therefore, we were ready to return home to America. However, we had mixed emotions.

As homesick as we were, and as much as we desired to get back home in Minnesota, when the time came for us to actually pack up and get ready to leave, it proved to be a very difficult task. We had twenty two regular students, and thirty part time students. They begged us to stay. John Quansa traveled from Kumasi. We told him we were leaving the college in very capable hands. But he said that was not the same. He said he had walked with Professor Gibson, and that no one could take our place. The last week before we were to leave, most of our full time students were at our house helping us pack. Every time we opened a suitcase or packed a box, their hands were there trying to help, but continuing to urge us not to leave. We explained to them that we were obligated and committed to return to Minnesota Bible College to teach there in the Fall. They did not seem to understand. They cried.

When we got into our car to drive to the airport, we all began to cry. We cried all of the way to the airport. When we arrived at the airport, we were met by Mr. Asmah, the Chief Customs Inspector for Ghana. He was crying too. We expected to have to open our bags and have them spread out over the terminal floor. But that didn't happen. Mr. Asmah put a chalk mark on our bags. Not a single bag was opened. He told us that he knew that we would not take advantage of our friendship. We thanked God for helping us to gain that kind of respect and trust. We boarded the very crowded Pan Am jet late that night. The heat and humidity was stifling, as our clothes stuck to our bodies. We arrived back at JFK airport early the next morning. After considerable difficulty getting through customs, we headed for a place to get some American food. The first thing we ordered was a chocolate milk shake and hamburger. They were delicious.

As we close this chapter, I want to share with you the experience that proved to be the most precious memory we took back to America with us.

The students and other friends had a farewell party for our family. They presented us with beautiful gifts that we knew represented great sacrifice. We learned that they had missed meals in order to express their love for us. They could not love without giving.

Christian Adjei was asked to give the farewell address. You may recall the circumstances that brought him to Ghana Christian College. He reminded us that the African people, and specifically the people of Ghana would not remember us because we were the founders of Ghana Christian College. He went on to say, "They would not remember Professor

Gibson, Mama and the children because the professor is a great scholar, even thought they appreciated his teaching very much." He continued, "They would not remember us because the professor was a great administrator." He added that they thought I was often too strict. And then he said, "We will remember the professor and Mama and the children *because they loved us too much!*" He repeated himself, *"They loved us too much!"*

We were called upon to make some sacrifices. But those words from Christian Adjei certainly made it "Worth Any Sacrifice". Is it possible to love too much? The Apostle Paul expressed "too much" kind of love in his letter to the Romans. He simply said what John 3:16 says. "For one will hardly die for a righteous man; though perhaps for the good man someone would dare even to die. But God demonstrates His own love toward us, in that while we were yet sinners, Christ died for us." Romans 5:8 Yes, indeed, God loves us too much! Romans 9:3 is an even greater example of "too much" kind of love. In a word, Paul says that he would be willing to give up his own salvation and burn in the fires of hell, if by so doing his Jewish brothers would be saved. This presents a problem with many theologians and others as well. They say it is not righteous for a person to wish such a thing. However, there is the answer to the problem. He *"could* wish it", but did not "will it." That is in God's hands. There is no greater love outside of John 16, than that which was expressed by the Apostle Paul in that passage of Scripture.,

Before we left Kumasi at the time of our last visit with the Christians from the Ashanti Territory, we had a beautiful communion service with them. The love expressed above is experienced every time we meet around the Lord's Table and partake of the

Lord's Supper. People should be asked, "When is the last time you saw a man die?" Every time we partake of the "loaf" and the "cup" we experience the love of God that placed Jesus on the cross for us.

When we were in China, we were not allowed to meet in groups of more than twelve at any time. We met in Normadeene's and my room at the Novetel Hotel in Beijing and had communion with several of the people who were there with us. The thought came to us that this was a time when we truly bonded with Christians from all over the world, for God's Holy Spirit is not separated by miles. It was a comforting feeling, just like in Kumasi, to know that "though we were absent in the flesh, we were present in the spirit, rejoicing in the steadfast faith" of our brothers and sisters in Christ, back home in America, and all over the world. Colossians 2:5. We remembered that "God loved us too much!"

I can think of no greater honor to be bestowed upon us for our labors in Ghana, than to be remembered by the epitaph, *"They loved us too much!"*

The Farwell Arch when you leave Ghana or
enter the airport terminal

Normadeene and the children ready to
board the Pan Am jet for America

Chapter XXX

BACK HOME IN MINNESOTA

We had Butterflies in our stomachs as our United Airlines 707 jet circled The International Airport in Minneapolis. We wondered if the Judds would be there to meet us. We were still thinking of our precious staff, students and friends in Ghana. What we did not realize is that we were about to experience a reverse culture-shock in adjusting to life back in America.

We had left "Preacher", our parrot, behind at JFK, as he had to be in quarantine for several days. Our un-accompanied baggage would arrive some time in the next month or so, as it was sent via surface vessel. We wondered what we would do about transportation, as we left our Mercury Comet with Cyril Simkins, who purchased it from us for a fair market price. Where would we live? Many such questions flooded our minds. In my paper, "So you want to be a Missionary." I give advice on how to prepare to go to a mission field. As I look back in retrospect, I think it may be just as valuables to know how to prepare for adjusting to returning to the normal, every day routine when one returns back home from the mission field. So, After going through the procedure demanded by Customs, etc. we walked out into the terminal that led to "Baggage Claim." There waiting for us was Bob and Clare Judd with their family. They will never know how wonderful it was to see them. Bob has since gone to be with Jesus. They had traveled to Minneapolis to see us off to Ghana. And now they were there to greet us upon our arrival back home.

They took us to the home of Ray and Jane Scott in South Minneapolis where we would stay for a few days before leaving for California to see our family there. Jane prepared a delicious meal, our first home cooked American style meal since leaving in May of 1966. It all seemed like a dream. The Judds and Scotts treated us like royalty. It was great to be back in America! The number one order of business was to find suitable transportation. We needed a car that was reliable, as California was a far piece to travel and we desired to get there worry free, safe and sound.

Bob Judd agreed to take me to the Ford Mercury dealer, who sold us the Comet we took with us to Africa. His name was Sam, and he had become a very close friend who was genuinely interested in our welfare. He had a keen interest in our mission in Africa. He was delighted to see me and suggested he had just the right automobile to meet our needs. It was a 1966 maroon Mercury Montclair. It was beautiful. It was a "Demonstrator" just like new. He sold it to me for his cost. It was ready to drive away. So after signing the necessary papers, and making a small down payment, I followed Bob Judd back to the Scotts. The family was very pleased with our new car. We often thought that Sam, the car dealer was one of God's angels due to the way he took such good care of us.

We traveled to California and had a wonderful reunion with our family there. Then, we traveled back to Minnesota, by way of Havre Montana. Jack Rampelberg and the Sixth Avenue Christian Church in Havre had served us well as our Forwarding Agent church. They were there for us all of the time we were in Ghana. They provided for our every need, outside of the bank draft that was supplied for us by our angel at the Barkley Bank in Kumasi. One of the ladies from the church had faithfully prepared a news letter to keep the people who were supporting our mission informed. Something exciting happened every day we were in Ghana, and we were faithful to provide the information necessary for the news letter. As I look back, I believe the most important thing a missionary can do is communicate with those who are supporting his mission so they know they are receiving the proper mileage from their missionary dollars.

As we drove back to Minneapolis, we wondered where we would find a suitable place to live. As you know, we sold our house in Crystal New Hope and left most of our furniture with the buyer. We would just about have to start from scratch as far as furniture was concerned. We stored a few personal items in a store room off of my office. We left a few things with my brother Harlow, mainly a beautiful old solid oak desk which G.H. Cachairas had given to me. Somehow, that got lost in the shuffle.

Suddenly, nothing seemed the same. We realize that our experience in Ghana had changed our lives, especially our priorities forever. However, it also seemed that people had changed. Things were just not the same. Even people had changed. This seemed especially true in my class room. This was not true of everybody, though. Our dear friends and colleagues, Howard and Florence Hayes opened their hearts and home to us while we were looking for a permanent place of residence. We have kept in close touch with these precious people through the years.

As you may recall, it was his strong voice that convinced "the powers to be" to give us an extra year of sabbatical leave, which made possible our accomplishing our mission in Ghana of establishing Ghana Christian College.

We found a place to live in Richfield, a suburb of Minneapolis, across from Metropolitan Stadium, where the Minnesota Vikings and the Minnesota Twins played their games at that time. Cindy, G.A. and Becky were enrolled in public schools, and to our delight, Gibby enrolled in Minnesota Bible College to enter some kind of specialized Christian service. I resumed my teaching duties at the college. Somehow, as suggested, it was not the same. There was a spirit of unrest in our hearts. I kept having flashbacks to my class room in Ghana. I could not get the looks on the faces of my students there as they begged us to stay. But most of all, the students were not the same. The Spirit of rebellion and protest of the late Sixties and Seventies could be felt in my class room. The students I had in Ghana had a tremendous hunger for the truth. They sacrificed to get their education. They did not have the educational helps that we in America take for granted. Many of them walked for miles to get to our campus there. I wondered, was it me, or was there an attitude that was in strong contrast to our Ghana Christian College students?

Mrs. Marshall, our school Librarian, informed me that several of the professors were making fun of the fact that I started every class with a prayer. They suggested that my classes were more like a "revival" and there was no place for that in a college class room. I never confronted any of them. I just continued teaching those who were there to learn how to be specialized servants of our Lord. I discussed my feelings with Herman Kooey, a former

Board Chairman of Minnesota Bible College and a prominent preacher. He was the evangelist who preached that first evangelistic meeting for the church in Circle Pines. At that time he was involved in selling real estate and suggested that if we had a home of our own and would settle down, the feeling of unrest would leave. We decided to give that a chance and found a house he had listed that we liked. Then it happened. Once again God stepped in and kept us from making a mistake that we would long regret. It happened the day we were to close on the house Herman Kooey had found for us. Our FHA loan had been approved. All that was left to close the deal was for us to meet with Herman that afternoon and sign the necessary papers.

I arrived at my office early that morning. As I sat there praying and contemplating the Day's activities, I got to thinking about our meeting with Herman Kooey to close the deal on our new house. A feeling a panic suddenly overwhelmed me. A still small voice said, "Do not buy that house." I struggled with the thought. What would Herman Kooey think? He had gone to much work making possible our buying the house. Now, I knew that for some unforeseen reason, we should not meet with Herman Kooey that afternoon.

As I sat there praying, Austin Reynolds, one of our school's custodians stuck his head into my office and inquired if everything was alright. I recounted to him the feeling of panic I was having in regard to closing the deal on the house. He suggested that I go with my gut feeling. He offered to open the business office door so I could call Herman Kooey and tell him I had decided not to close the deal on the house. At that time we could not afford to have phones in our private offices, so I took advantage of Austin's kindness.

Understandably, Herman "blew his stack", so to speak, as I told him we would not meet with him that afternoon to close the deal on the house. Yes, I can understand his feelings, as he had spent much time and effort, and would also lose his commission on the house,

I drove home after class and informed Normadeene we were not going to meet with Herman Kooey to close on the house. After explaining to her the reason, she agreed that the timing was not right. Whenever we face important decisions throughout our marriage, we usually climb into our car and go for a ride, if for no other reason, just to clear our minds. We decided to go for a ride around beautiful Lake Minnetonka.

As we were enjoying the beauty of lake Minnetonka, we recalled the visit we had made to Urbana, Illinois to raise funds to help pay off our travel expenses for our return from Ghana. We spoke at The Webber Street Church of Christ where Bob and Clare Judd and their family attended. Bob was an elder of the church at that time. While we were there, we met Dr. Stan Smith who was instrumental in establishing a campus ministry at the University of Illinois in Champaign-Urbana. After hearing me speak, he was convinced that he needed someone like me to work with him in his campus ministry. He suggested that if we were ever interested, to let him know. We never gave it much serious thought after that.

Normadeene suddenly remarked, "I wonder how that campus ministry is doing down in Champaign-Urbana? We ought to give Stan Smith a call some time and give him a word of encouragement." We both thought he was having a wonderful ministry and doing a wonderful work on that university campus. We left it at that.

When we pulled into our parking place back home, our telephone was ringing. Fortunately we were able to get to the phone in time. It was John Pierce, Senior Minister of the Webber Street Church where we had spoken, and also Chairman of the Board of Christian Campus Foundation at the University of Illinois.

He started by saying that what he was about to propose may be impossible, but after much prayer on the part of the members of the campus ministries board, he decided to give me a call. He proceeded to tell me that they had been praying for a man to take the place of Stan Smith who had resigned from his campus ministry there, and that my name kept coming up as the man for the job.

I spoke to Normadeene and shared with her the nature of the call. We both stood there in shock. If we had closed the deal on that house we could not have even considered the campus ministry at the University of Illinois. I did not relate to John Pierce what had happened, but I did tell him that because of something that happened to me that morning, if they were willing to pay my plane fare from Chicago to Champaign-Urbana, on my way back from a "Faith Promise" in Owasso, Michigan, I would be willing to meet with them and consider the possibility of becoming their campus minister. They needed somebody with experience with Internationals, and also someone qualified to teach in the Religious Studies program at the university.

They agreed to my conditions. After meeting with the Christian Campus Foundation Board, I was convinced that God's strong hand was upon us once again. He sent Austin Reynolds as His angel to open the door to the college office so I could call Herman Kooey and cancel our appointment with him. Once again, had we purchased that house, we never could have accepted the call to the campus ministry in Illinois, and God's history book, "The twenty-ninth chapter of Acts" would be greatly altered. Once again, "Man proposes, but it is God who disposes."

We accepted the call they gave to us on the condition that I would be released from my contract with Minnesota Bible College which I had signed several months earlier. I approached President Skinner and Dean Grice with my desire to accept the call to Illinois. They both said they did not like it, but lamented they should not stand in the way of God's will. President Skinner told me that if I could get the Chairman of the Board, Bruce Miller to release me from my contract, he would reluctantly give me his blessing. Bruce Miller responded in the same way as President Skinner and Dean Grice. We immediately called John Pierce and told him we would accept the call to be the first full time campus minister for the Christian Campus Foundation. Stan Smith served on a part time basis, as he was a professor in the Agriculture Department at the university.

The most difficult situation we faced, was to inform the student body of our decision to leave Minnesota Bible College. We had become very close to them and especially with some of the groups we traveled with to promote the program of the college. The Victors Quartet was especially affected. Many of them cried when we told them of our decision.

President Skinner told me that I was going to have to make the announcement about our decision. It so happened, that the day I was to make may announcement, the student body dedicated the College Year Book to our family in honor of our work in Africa.

As difficult at it was to leave the college, we now realize that all that had gone before was to prepare us for what was yet to come. We were glad that we "hung on to our forks". In our next book we will share with you our experiences in the Seventies that brought our nation to the place it is today, after Nine-One-One. We have enjoyed sharing this part of our lives with you that take us up to 1968. We will now begin to recount our experiences with angels during the past forty years of our lives. Yes, once again we urge you to "save your fork", for the best is yet to come!

Oh! by the way, I don't want to get ahead of myself, but I did return to Kumasi, the place of human sacrifice, with its mysterious vine covered mausoleum, just outside the city, on the road to Afrancho in the summer of 1991. However, I was not able to gain safe passage into that mysterious mausoleum, on the road to Afrancho.

Apendix

Due to the numerous responses of men and women who have been inspired by the challenge of Promise Keepers and other evangelistic outreaches, to become missionaries to the unreached peoples of the world, we are adding this appendix that presents valuable principles and guidelines for becoming a foreign missionary. It would have been very beneficial to us to have this information before we went to Ghana. We could have escaped some of the dangers and pitfalls we faced had we been forewarned and thereby forearmed. We have prepared the following guidelines which have been beneficial to many with whom we have shared them.

So You Want To Be A Missionary?

(Isaiah 6: 1-8)

INTRODUCTION:

1. Definition: "Missionary"—from the Latin "To send."
2. Closely associated with the words "Apostle" (Apo-Stello)-Greek "Send" and "From".
3. Jesus was the greatest of all "Missionaries". There are three kinds in the Bible.
4. Missionaries or Apostles of God. Jesus was "sent from God",(Gal. 4:4)
   John the Baptist was also "sent from God", (John 1:6)
5. There were "Missionaries" or "Apostles "of the Church. Paul and Barnabas were "Missionary Apostles" of the Antioch Church. Acts 13:1-3)
6. There were "Missionary Apostles" of Christ. This included The Twelve and Matthias. (Acts 1:21 &22 tells the special qualifications for being an "Apostle of Christ,") The Apostle Paul was a special Apostle to the Gentiles. (Acts 9)
7. Jesus recognized three things:

   (1) The lostness of the lost. (Revelation 21:8)
   (2) The Power of the Gospel to save. (Romans 1:16)
   (3) His part in saving the lost. (Luke 19:10)

225

8. Jesus' mission was unique in that it was revealed in all of its aspects.

  (1) His purpose—"to seek and to save the lost". Luke 19:10.

  (2) His task—"As the Father has sent me, so send I you." John 20:21

  (3) Message—"Go into all the world and preach *the Gospel.*" Mark 16:16.

9. A young man asked his preacher, "What can I do for Jesus? He was told, "Go where He has not been. Go where He is not, and take Him with you."

10. With that in mind, a good definition for a missionary in our day and age is one:

  (1) Who will go were he has not been,

  (2) To do what he has not done,

  (3) With money he does not have.

11. Our family did just that in 1966 as we traveled to Ghana, West Africa to establish a Bible College for training African evangelists, preachers and teachers.

12. There are many things we did not know that would have been very helpful to us. That is why we have put together this paper, "So you want to be a missionary?"

13. Even, though times have changed, basic principles have not changed. This paper is intended to help young missionary recruits understand more fully what will be required of them both on and off of the mission field, and help them to prepare themselves for the

eventuality of hearing God ask, "Who will I send, and who will go for us?", so they can intelligently reply, "Here am I, send me!"

The following are things to consider before entering a mission field:

I. CAN GOD USE ME AS A MISSSIONARY?

A. Am I qualified and prepared for the mission field?

(1) Spiritually: Hebrews 5:11-6:10.
(2) Mentally: (Emotionally stable) (Effect on family members)
(3) Physically: (Natives equate physical ailments with spiritual weakness.)
(4) Administrative: (Successful at home— Experience-proven self.)

II. PREPARING FOR THE MISSION FIELD:

A. Where will my field of service be?

(1) Where is the greatest need for my specific talents?
(2) Where does my greatest interest lie?

B. Choosing a Forwarding Agent. (Will make or break missionary)

(1) What kind of person or persons must I look for?
(2) What will his or her duties be?

C. How will I raise the necessary financial support?

(1)   Decide on basis of appeal. (Few large churches or many small churches and individuals?)

(2)   Decide upon amount needed for living and service links.

(3)   Arrange itinerary of speaking engagements after thoroughly acquainting self with the field of service you have chosen and the nature of your mission. (Always be ready to answer the question, "What is your mission?")

D. The battle of the Visas.

(1)   Obtaining passports and fulfilling medical requirements.

(a) Sending applications along with birth certificates, along with three passport size photos.

(b) Obtaining immunity cards from health authorities and making arrangements for necessary shots. (Find out which shots are necessary for the country you desire to enter)

(2)   Obtaining Visas and Entry Permits.

(a) Send visa application with three passport size photos to Principal Immigration officer along with a letter of invitation from the church or organization holding the missionary quota under which you are to enter the country.

(b) Instruct those on the mission field to keep in close contact with the authorities while your visas are being processed.

III. *HOW WILL I TRAVEL TO THE MISSION FIELD?*

1. Air, land or Sea?—Advantages and disadvantages?
2. Which route will I travel? Direct or by way of cultural centers?
3. Seek most economical fare possible. (Do this far in advance)
4. What will I take with me to the mission field?

   (a) Make a list of necessities.
   (b) Contact those who have been there for advice.

      (1) What will be available on the mission field?
      (2) Which will be the most expensive? Bring with or buy on the field if available.

5. Packing for the mission field.

   (a) Personal or professional?

      (1) Investigate requirements. (Size, waterproofing, etc.)

6. Shipping to the mission field.

   (a) Contact shipping firm
   (b) Be sure to have Bill of Lading sent to you long before goods arrive on the field.

(c) Be able to list all unaccompanied baggage.

(d) Do not bring any fire arms into the country.

(e) Investigate as to the amount of duty required for entry of various possessions. (Obtain necessary unnumbered licenses.)

(f) Have mission field apply for "Free Gift" certificate for anything coming to be used as public rather than private property.

7. What money shall I take with me to the mission field?

(a) Take travelers checks to cover expenses of hotels, food, cabs and general living from home to the field.

(b) Upon entering various countries where you expect to visit a few days, have enough money exchanged to cover above expenses.

(c) Take enough money with you to cover immediate expenses upon arrival on the field.

(1) Rent Advances often required. (Do I want a furnished or unfurnished house?)

(2) House furnishing: Things I will not receive from home.

(d) Tax and Duty—Expect to pay at least $5,000.00 to bring any vehicle into the country that does not qualify under "Free Gift" act. (Used articles are taxed much less than new articles.)

IV. *ARRIVING ON THE MISSION FIELD.*

    A.   When and where will I arrive?

        (1) Notify authorities of sponsoring organizations as to the time and place of entry. (Have them prepare a place for you to stay for the first few days.)

        (2) Be absolutely certain that your message is received.

    B.   Procedure upon entering the country.

        (l)   You must show your passport and visa immediately upon entering the country. (Visa and Entry Permit may be waiting for you at the Port of Entry)

        (2) You must declare all currency and checks brought into the country with you.(Keep your copy of this entry in a safe place as you will need it when you leave the country to get an Exit Visa.)

        (3) Have Immunity record to show health authorities.

    C. Declare *all* unaccompanied baggage. (Be sure to declare an adequate number of packages. (Better too many than not enough.—usually three months is allowed for inspection of unaccompanied baggage.)

    D. Pass to have accompanied baggage inspected. (You will be asked your occupation and whether you have liquor or cigarettes in luggage)

    E. You may now greet those whom you came to serve that have come to greet and welcome you into their midst.

V. *ON THE MISSION FIELD*

A. Greeting the Brethren.

    (1) Have a short speech prepared.

B. The Brethren greet you.
C. Where will I live? (Establish base of operation}

    (1) Decide where is the best place for the mission you have come to accomplish.
    (2) Try to avoid unnecessary jealousy in the regard. (This is accomplished by explaining the reasons for choosing a particular geographical location.)

D. Adjusting to the cultural shock.

    (1) Be very patient with yourself and your mission.
    (2) Previous preparation by reading and becoming familiar with the culture and customs of the people you have come to serve will be very helpful at this time. (Why I attended the U. of Ghana)
    (3) Learn the monetary system as well as social customs as soon as possible.
    (4) Establish a time schedule as soon as possible. (Budget out time)

        (a) Adjust your pace to the field you are in, giving particular attention to the climate.
        (b) Provide time for conducting necessary business activities.
        (c) Provide time for recreation and relaxation with your family.

(d) Provide time to accomplish your mission on the field.

(e) Remember that "Rome was not built in a day".

(5). Establish wholesome and regular eating habits.

(a) Visit stores and markets to see what is available.

(b) Be careful of locally grown vegetables. (With proper care and preparation they can be valuable and inexpensive.)

(c) Remember, good eating habits are necessary for good health. If you are going to economize, this is *NOT* the place to do it.

(d) Give particular attention to your water supply. You may have to boil water for human consumption. (This is something to consider when deciding where to live.)

E.   Financial matters on the Mission field.

(1)   Establish a Personal Bank Account.

(a) This is necessary for the exchange of money as well as for expedience sake in paying your bills.

(b) Inquire about a personal remittance quota. (This will require the paying of income tax, but will enable you to take money out of the country at the time of departure. (You must decide upon a figure to declare as "personal income".)

(2) Establishing a General Missions account.

    (a) This requires a "letter of credit" and "power of attorney from your supporting churches or Forwarding Agent. (Funds are transferred from your U.S. missions account)

    (b) As soon as possible learn well the currency and coins of the country. This could save you many dollars.

F. Pitfalls to Avoid on the Mission Field.

(1) Do not come as "The Great White Benefactor." (Let it be known that your mission is *spiritual*, not *material*.)

(2) Do not make any promises that you may later decide not to keep.

(3) Do not set any precedence that could later become a skeleton in the closet that will come out and haunt you.

(4) Do not show any form of favoritism. Jealousy can raise up its ugly green head and spoil your influence among the people.

(5) Do not do for the people *anything* that they better be able to do for themselves.

(6) Do not subsidize the programs of the churches.

(7) Do not offer to pay the preachers.

(8) Do not become a dictator. *Command*, but do not *demand* respect.

(9) Do not become too "familiar" with any of the people.

(10) Do not discuss "personal problems" with
      your people. (Avoid any family disputes
      in the presence of the people.)

(I1) Do not try to Americanize or Europeanize,
      or impose your culture on them.
      Christianity is adaptable to every culture.
      In many instances their culture is better
      than ours.

VI. *LEAVING THE MISSION FIELD.*

A.   When to leave a Mission Field.

(l)   Determine the time you intend to spend
      on the mission field before entering the
      field if possible.

(2)   When to return will be governed by how
      long you stay and by the pre-set goals
      you have been able to accomplish.

(3)   Terms of duty as well as over-all mission
      service on a given field should be
      determined. (Average life of missionary
      in Africa in Nineteenth Century was five
      years)

(4)   A target date should be fixed for a
      complete withdrawal of mission support.
      (This may be done by a gradual process.)

(5)   A list of goals to be accomplished on the
      field should be established, and when
      these goals are accomplished, the
      missionary should leave. (Paul did this-
      never stayed longer three years.)

(6)   One's goal should be an *"INDIGENOUS"*
      church in every phase of the churches'
      life and ministry.

B.   How to leave the Mission Field?

    (1)   Leave with faith and confidence in the people in whom you have invested your life.

    (2)   Leave with faith and confidence in the fact that you have done your best with what God has placed in your hands. (Parable of talents)

    (3)   Leave with a feeling of love and respect for the people who remain on the mission field.

    (4)   Leave before you become a problem on the mission field yourself.

RELATIONSHIP OF MISSIONARY TO THE CHURCH

(The Church is the Missionaries Life Line)

1.   Keep open the lines of communication. (Communication is the key to understanding, and understanding is the key to healthy relationships.)

    (a)   Lack of communication by not providing regular detailed financial and progress reports is the number one criticism of missionaries.

2.   There is a great need for a responsible body to care for the needs of the people on the mission field

    (a)   Everybody's business is nobody's business.

    (b)   Provide a financial "safety valve". (Ill. of Mr. Matani and check)

3. There needs to be a program of promotion for the mission while the missionary is on the field.
4. When the missionary arrives home he can do much toward encouraging the churches by sharing his experiences with them.(People need this)
5. There should be a relationship of mutual trust and confidence.(This would help avoid many problems at home and abroad. Missionaries should put their best foot forward. Keep speaking engagements. Prepare challenging reports etc.)

Conclusion

"Go where He is not." "Go where He is not and take Him with you." Very few people read the 'Four Gospels'. They read 'The *Fifth Gospel*', our lives.

As you learned from *Angels In Africa,* Normadeene and I attempted to use these guidelines when we were in Ghana. Now after all of these years, we find many of the principles contained in this paper are very relevant to our present age. The circumstances may be different, but the need for the Gospel and the teachings of Jesus Christ have not changed. They are Divine absolutes.

We have often admonished our children with the saying, "A person's intelligence is in direct proportion to his or her ability to adjust themselves to the situation at hand." That is certainly true today. The mission field calls for flexibility and much adjustment to the situations one faces on a daily basis. This can and must be done without compromising any basic biblical principles.

We have experienced almost every area of Christian ministry. We have been in local pastorates. We have been in new church evangelism. We have been a professor in a Bible college.

We have been in The Campus Ministry on three great college campuses. We have been President of a Christian college. We have been foreign missionaries to Africa and China. All of this has served us well to share our experience and knowledge of the mission field with you. It is important to point out that the "mission field" is not separated by geographical boundaries.

Where ever there is a soul to be saved is a mission field. In our eagerness to save the lost in foreign lands, we must not forget that we have a nation of our own that is in dire need of salvation.

Our hope and prayer for those who read this paper is that whenever and wherever our Lord may call, you will be ready to "Go where He has not been and take Him with you", as you respond with Isaiah of old, "Here am I, send me!"